Hello,

Even if you're not a fan of journaling or you don't have the time for it, many experts have confirmed the benefits of keeping a journal during pregnancy. Here are some of the reasons why you should start writing as soon as your baby bump begins to show.

1. **Reduce Stress**

    Finding an outlet for your thoughts during pregnancy, can help you find solutions to your pregnancy fears and manage the anxiety that comes from negative thoughts. It's an effective means to access your emotions and rid yourself of stress, which may affect the wellbeing of your baby

2. **Organize Yourself**

    We know how disoriented a pregnancy can make expecting mothers feel. It's no easy task getting everything ready for the little pink feet, maintaining a healthy lifestyle as well as managing your regular schedule. Apart from organizing your thoughts, journaling can also help to coordinate your duties, manage your time efficiently and ultimately make you a more productive mum-to-be.

3. **Track Your Progress**

It is a lot of fun tracking your pregnancy and recording the way your baby bump has grown week by week. Journaling a pregnancy can also act as a confidence booster. Your journal will be an inventory of your achievements and successes during your pregnancy.

4. **Celebrate Your Happy Moments**

    How did you feel when you first found out that it was a boy or a girl? What was your first reaction when you saw the ultrasound image of your baby? Describe these positive emotions in your journal. At the end of each day, write down all the things that went smoothly and that you're proud of.

So, get your **"My Weekly Pregnancy Journal"** in PDF format for free by clicking the link below:

https://harleycarrparenting.com/from-baby-bump-all-the-way-to-babys-birthday

or

Print the document and start to make your own pregnancy Journal week by week.

From Your Baby Bump To Your Baby´s First Birthday

Learn What Happens Before and After the Birth of Your Baby - So You Are Prepared and Confident During Pre and Postnatal Development

Harley Carr

© **Copyright 2019 - All rights reserved.**

The content contained within this book may not be reproduced, duplicated or transmitted without direct written permission from the author or the publisher.

Under no circumstances will any blame or legal responsibility be held against the publisher, or author, for any damages, reparation, or monetary loss due to the information contained within this book, either directly or indirectly.

Legal Notice:

This book is copyright protected. It is only for personal use. You cannot amend, distribute, sell, use, quote or paraphrase any part, or the content within this book, without the consent of the author or publisher.

Disclaimer Notice:

Please note the information contained within this document is for educational and entertainment purposes only. All effort has been executed to present accurate, up to date, reliable, complete information. No warranties of any kind are declared or implied. Readers acknowledge that the author is not engaging in the rendering of legal, financial, medical or professional advice. The content within this book has been derived from various sources. Please consult a licensed professional before attempting any techniques outlined in this book.

By reading this document, the reader agrees that under no circumstances is the author responsible for any losses, direct or indirect, that are incurred as a result of the use of information contained within this document, including, but not limited to, errors, omissions, or inaccuracies.

This printable "My Weekly Pregnancy Journal" has 38 pages where you can track the fruit-like size of your baby from 4 weeks throughout 40 weeks.

Now, you can have your *own* "Weekly Pregnancy Journal " in just one click away!

Let´s get started ...

Enjoy and Best Wishes to your Pregnancy Journey!

Harley Carr

Table of Contents

Introduction	**11**
Part 1: Prenatal Development—The Nine-Month Journey	**23**
Chapter 1: The First Trimester (1-3 Months)	**25**
The First Month	25
The Second Month	31
The Third Month	36
Chapter 2: The Second Trimester (4-6 Months)	**43**
The Fourth Month	43
The Fifth Month	50
The Sixth Month	55
Chapter 3: The Third Trimester (7-9 Months)	**61**
The Seventh Month	61
The Eighth Month	67
The Ninth Month	73
Part 2: Baby's First Year—Milestones and Mental Leaps	**79**
Chapter 4: 1st Month-3rd Month	**81**
First Month	81
Second Month	90
Third Month	98

Chapter 5: 4th Month-6th Month — 107

    Fourth Month — 108
    Fifth Month — 116
    Sixth Month — 124

Chapter 6: 7th Month-9th Month — 133

    Seventh Month — 133
    Eighth Month — 141
    Ninth Month — 149

Chapter 7: 10th Month-12th Month — 159

    Tenth Month — 160
    Eleventh Month — 170
    Twelfth Month — 179

Chapter 8: 10 Mental Leaps in Your Baby's Life — 187

    Mental Leap 1 — 188
    Mental Leap 2 — 189
    Mental Leap 3 — 191
    Mental Leap 4 — 192
    Mental Leap 5 — 194
    Mental Leap 6 — 195
    Mental Leap 7 — 197
    Mental Leap 8 — 198
    Mental Leap 9 — 200
    Mental Leap 10 — 201

Conclusion — 203

References — 207

Introduction

Pregnancy is a fascinating experience that gives you an opportunity to learn something new almost every single day. While your body is changing from the inside out, there are several things that are happening that you are likely unaware of. A lot of mothers do not feel that they have enough knowledge or education on the various stages of development while their baby is still in the womb. While this isn't necessarily a problem, it can impact your confidence for when the baby is born. By knowing exactly what is going on during your given stage of pregnancy, you will feel better equipped to handle anything that comes your way as a parent.

Knowing how big your baby is each week can provide you with some insight as to how they are developing as well as why your body is feeling the way that it is. As pregnancy progresses, the body needs to literally shift internally in order to make room for the growing baby. As this happens, you will feel a wide variety of various symptoms. You might also be genuinely curious as to how big your baby is getting and how fast this process is taking place. One minute, you aren't showing at all and the next you have a bump that prevents you from being able to see your toes.

As your baby is growing inside the womb, you must wait patiently until the day that you finally get to deliver them in order to truly see them for the first time. Ultrasounds will hold you over until then, but there is nothing like being able to hold and see your baby with your own eyes for the first time. Once you give birth, all of your parenting worries and curiosities become intensified because you have your baby before you. If you felt like there were a lot of unanswered questions during your pregnancy, these are likely going to carry over into your baby's infant stage. This is why it is important to obtain this knowledge before the baby is born.

The main problem is that most parents do not know what the typical milestones are for their babies. They also do not realize that each baby is going to develop at a different rate of speed, and that is okay. Much like you are an individual with unique traits and your own personality, so is your baby. Though much tinier, your little human is going to develop at the rate that is natural to them. While there are some things that you can do to guide them toward the healthiest choices in life, most of what parenting involves is being able to accept the unpredictable and just go with the flow.

Real Solutions

Most pregnancy guides will simply state obvious facts that aren't hard to research on your own. This one is different because it will provide you with tried and true solutions that you can apply to your own life. Your baby will benefit from this useful information that you learn, and your confidence will continue to grow daily. From the instant of conception, you will learn all that you need to know regarding your baby's development. By the time you give birth, you will feel fully prepared and capable to be the best parent that you can be.

Some of the topics covered are:

- Week-by-week prenatal development
- Development of the senses
- Accurate gender identification
- What to expect in the first year of life (milestones)

You are going to feel knowledgeable and ready to guide your baby through each stage of development. What a child needs is a parent who takes action and has solutions. This is what this guide aims to provide you with. Though your solutions might need backup plans at times, it is better to have some ideas than to enter blindly. Parenting can be an unpredictable job, but it is one that can be very rewarding once you start to figure it out for yourself.

There will be no need to panic or wonder if you are doing the right thing because this guide is filled with real solutions to real problems that are faced by many daily. It is going to provide you with a way to track your baby's progress to ensure that everything is going well developmentally, cognitively, emotionally, and physically. By knowing what the standard rate of development is, you will be able to notice any patterns if something goes wrong. Instead of panicking and not knowing how to handle the problem, you will be able to get to your doctor quickly, providing your child with a faster solution.

My Story

My name is Harley Carr, and I'm a mother just like you. My three children mean the world to me, but raising them has provided me with just any many challenges as there were triumphs. With them currently aged 8, 5, and 3, I definitely have my hands full. The first year of a child's life is always one of the most chaotic for the mother.

There are so many decisions to be made, ones that can shape the future of their lives forever. It is a lot of pressure when you truly think about it.

One of the biggest decisions I faced was whether to return to work or stay home with my newborn. My son, Jaden, was my first child. Luckily, I have a very supportive partner who told me that I should stay at home with the baby so that we could further bond. My partner knew how much I yearned to get out of the office and into the nursery. Since my pregnancy was filled with days of never-ending nausea and contractions that nearly made me pass out, he thought that I would benefit from just taking some time to be with the baby.

It was the best decision I ever made. I stayed at home with Jaden, and for his first year of life, I learned from all of our trials and tribulations. It was through this time with him that I decided I would breastfeed all of my children. Jaden was a very healthy baby, and he latched on right away—I felt so proud in that moment. He wasn't too fussy, but boy did he hate bath time. Through all of these experiences, I truly believe I became a better mother. I was as educated as possible, but there was still so much to learn. Jaden taught me everything else that I needed to know to raise him and his siblings.

Through all the diaper changes and baths given in the last 8 years, I feel that my knowledge can also help you. Whether you plan on becoming a stay-at-home mom or must return to the workforce shortly after delivery, you will be ready for the milestones to come. Instead of struggling, you can learn from my struggles. With the tips that I provide you and the methods that I share, not only will you feel prepared, but you will feel excited to guide your child through their first year of life.

The Benefits

There are countless parenting books to read, so you might be wondering, why this one? The answer is simple—you need a complete picture of how your baby is going to develop, and this book will provide you with one. I will cover the time spent inside the womb to the first year of your baby's active life, so you will know and understand exactly what is going on both physically and mentally. There is so much that can change every single week, from the time that you first find out you are pregnant to actually being a mother of a one-year-old. The progress never stops, so this means you need to keep up.

This book will actually allow you to feel that you are ahead of the game. Instead of struggling to catch up, you will be prepared and able to handle anything that comes your way. Being a great mom has nothing to do with getting everything right on the first try. It actually involves a lot of trial and error, which a lot of people do not realize is very normal for parenting the first year of a child's life. As long as you have good intentions with the desire to put in as much effort as possible, you are going to be great as a parent. Plus, if you have a supportive partner to help you, then your baby is going to have twice as much support throughout their life.

While it isn't possible to be worry-free parents at all times, having this knowledge will put you at ease in the times when you need it most. When a baby is crying but cannot tell you what is wrong, this can be one of the most intimidating moments of your entire life. Your natural instinct as a parent will likely kick in, trying to come up with solutions for your distressed baby, but there will be times when you just can't seem to figure it out. Don't forget to take care of yourself, to breathe. Your baby is going to be picking up on your energy, positive or negative.

This book will not only shed some light on the topics you normally wonder about, but it will also remind you that your approach and attitude are super important parts of parenting. The energy that you put out is going to be reflected right back at you. When your baby can sense that you are okay, they will also feel that they can be okay. Starting from the very beginning, you are that baby's entire support system. From developing in the womb to experiencing the first year of life, your baby will be relying on you to lead the way.

Why Is It Important?

Do you want to know that your baby is developing well?

Are you curious about what milestones you can expect?

Have you ever wondered what your baby is mentally capable of understanding?

All of these questions (and more) will be answered by the time you are finished with this guide. Not only will you have the answers that you need, but you will also have proven knowledge on the topics that will guide you toward making your own decisions as you explore the various joys of parenthood.

If you feel ready to become a great parent, don't delay in reading this guide. Though you might only be a few weeks pregnant, now is the perfect time to sit down and learn all that there is to know about your baby's developmental stages. As you progress, you can follow along in the book to see exactly where you stand and where your baby compares to the average statistics.

Any delays are only going to hold you back from becoming the best parent you can be and that will mean that you have to figure out the answers to important questions after your baby has already been born. You are going to learn that you have the ability to multitask like never before, yet it is still going to be easier to take care of a baby when you already have all of the knowledge stored in your memory. Waiting until the end of your pregnancy, or even after delivery, is only going to hinder your own progress.

No parent wants to feel unprepared, so you shouldn't put yourself in that situation. It can be confusing and very overwhelming to feel this way. Give yourself and your baby the advantage of a proper education. Read this guide several times if you need to, studying different sections if you feel that you need a refresher at any given time. This guide is much more than just information that you will benefit from. Think about it as a way for you to navigate through parenting while always being able to remain calm since the answers can be found as long as you keep on reading.

Part 1: Prenatal Development—The Nine-Month Journey

As you become familiar with the term prenatal development, you will realize that each trimester of your baby's life during your pregnancy is going to be different. There will be a lot of symptoms that you will feel externally, but your baby is also going to be experiencing many changes inside of the womb. Through all nine months of your pregnancy, you are going to be amazed at all that can happen in this amount of time. From a small embryo to a fully-developed infant, you are going to learn about each milestone along the way.

Chapter 1: The First Trimester (1-3 Months)

A lot changes within the first trimester of your pregnancy. Though you can't see it and you might not feel it very much, your baby is developing at a rapid rate of speed. During this time, you are likely preparing your own life for the arrival of your new bundle of joy. This can include a change in lifestyle, tightening up on finances, and planning a nursery design in your home. Prenatal development actually starts upon conception, and it does not end until your baby is born. Through these nine months, you are going to learn a lot about yourself and a lot about your baby.

The First Month

During your first month of pregnancy, your baby is a tiny embryo made up of cells. Though your baby is still microscopic, there are actually two layers of cells present, called the epiblast and the hypoblast. These cells are all going to develop into your baby's systems and parts that will continue growing throughout your pregnancy. Comparing its size to something you are used to seeing, your baby is no larger than a poppy seed at this point in the pregnancy. It is amazing, however, to think about how quickly they are developing at this stage.

When you first conceive your baby, a small ball of cells settles into your uterus. It will then split up into two groups, half forming your baby and the other half forming the placenta. As you may know, the placenta will begin to form once you are pregnant and it will house your baby like a protective barrier. In the beginning, the placenta starts out as a yolk sac. This sac is what produces blood for your baby, the embryo. As the placenta develops, it will also provide a way to remove waste and bring in nutrients. Think about it as your baby's lifeline, connected to you for support.

Though the embryo is tiny, it is still very powerful. During this time, the amniotic sac will also start to form. Think about this as a bag of water that surrounds the baby, providing it with proper fluids. It will later become incorporated into your baby's digestive tract. Eventually, the third layer of cells will emerge. The first is the inner layer that is known as the endoderm. This part becomes the digestive system, lungs, and liver. The mesoderm is the middle layer, and it becomes your baby's heart, bones, muscles, sex organs, and kidneys. The final layer is the ectoderm. This is what forms your baby's skin, eyes, hair, and nervous system.

Your Changes

Though the symptoms might be slight, you will notice some definite changes in the way that you feel. As soon as one week after conception, your body will know that some big changes are about to take place. Most of the time, you are going to be oblivious to all of this. Even those who are actively trying to get pregnant will typically not be able to confirm if they are indeed housing an embryo at this point or not. Some of the earliest pregnancy symptoms can mirror PMS symptoms. This can be confusing because experiencing PMS symptoms each month is likely a normal occurrence. The cramps that you feel won't likely faze you, and the mood swings will probably seem normal.

There might be some bloating, but that will likely be attributed to normal PMS behavior that you are used to each month. No matter if you are feeling anything in abundance or not at all, it is likely still too early to be able to rely on an at-home pregnancy test to deliver the news that you are waiting for. If you are pregnant, the fertilized egg and the uterus make contact within the very first week. This is when your baby will attach itself to your uterine lining. Though there is nothing to physically indicate to you that this is happening inside, a lot of women just seem to know when it is taking place.

If you notice some bleeding, this is normal. A lot of women are discouraged when they see bleeding because this is usually an indication of their period starting. Ironically, this bleeding can happen when the baby implants. It is known as implantation bleeding, and up to 25% of women experience it. The way to differentiate it from your period will be the timing and the color. This bleeding typically happens earlier than your period, and it will be a lot lighter in color. Whether it is pink, red, or brown, it should still be lighter than period blood.

Again, bloating can occur during this time, maybe even a little bit of abdominal pressure. Your breasts can also feel tender to the touch. Most of this is still normal for a lot of women when they are experiencing PMS. After the first 6-12 days of fertilization, your body will begin producing the hormone known as HCG. This is what at-home pregnancy tests can pick up on. HCG is what tells your body to produce progesterone and estrogen in order to nourish the cells until the placenta takes over (usually at around 8 weeks).

If you suspect you are pregnant, but it is too early for testing, the best thing you can do is take care of yourself. Be easy on yourself and get a lot of rest. Making sure that you are getting enough vitamin D is also essential. Take a prenatal vitamin if you haven't started already. Try to avoid toxic situations, like places where a lot of smoking will be taking place. Ingesting secondhand smoke puts your baby in great danger. As for eating, know that healthy fat is good fat. You and your baby are both going to need it as your baby continues to grow. Eat foods that are rich in omega fatty acids, like eggs and avocados.

If you need to get up and moving, go for a swim! Swimming is a great and safe low-impact way to exercise if you are pregnant or think you might be pregnant. It also allows for many cardiovascular benefits that will keep you healthy and in shape. Though your belly is going to grow, this does not mean that you need to sit around doing nothing all day. Being active is great for your body, your baby, and your mental health. Getting low-impact exercise into your schedule 3-4 times a week is a great thing. Go on walks, take a few dips in the pool, and do what makes you feel good as your body undergoes this first month of changes.

The Second Month

At this stage in your pregnancy, your baby should be around the size of a raspberry. This is a big difference from the cluster of cells that they were just a month earlier. Your baby's eyes are forming during this point, and though you won't know the color just yet, the retinas are well on their way to development. The same can be said for your baby's sex organs. Though it is still very early on in the pregnancy, your baby is currently developing in this way. In a few weeks' time, an ultrasound will be able to let you know if you are expecting a baby boy or baby girl.

It can be hard to estimate exactly how big your baby is during the second month, but most experts say that they can be anywhere from ½ inch to ¾ inch. The average growth rate is around a millimeter a day, which is astounding to think about. This growth is not only limited to height. It can also include growth spurts in various parts of your baby's body, like their limbs or back. If you were able to take a close-up look at your baby, you would see that they now have eyelids, lips, and a nose. Their hands and feet are still webbed, soon to be separated.

By the end of this week, your baby's systems and essential organs have begun to develop. In this tiny embryo, there is now a tiny heart, brain, liver, kidneys, and so on. They will continue to grow and develop quickly as you progress in your pregnancy. After the second month, a lot of mothers agree that time seems to go by very quickly and many developmental milestones are reached in short proximity to one another. Most doctors would agree that, during this stage, your baby starts looking more baby-like and less reptilian.

Their heartbeat is around 150-170 beats per minute. This is still about twice as fast as your own heart rate. While you might not be able to feel them just yet, your baby is able to make spontaneous movements. As your baby's growth progresses, so does the rate in which your amniotic fluid increases. This makes your womb bigger, making even more space for the growing baby that you have inside your belly. As your baby grows and grows, this space also becomes larger. This is why the size of your belly begins to show shortly after the second month of pregnancy. Typically, women have the infamous "baby bump" during their third month, but all women are different. You can have a perfectly healthy pregnancy, yet not be showing at all.

Your Changes

Even if you aren't showing just yet, your body is still likely feeling all of the impacts of having a growing baby inside of it. Your morning sickness might be hitting you pretty hard at this point. Though your baby is still tiny, remember that your uterus is still rapidly expanding to keep up with all of the growth that is taking place. Your uterus itself has likely expanded to the size of a large grapefruit by now. This is what can be causing your morning sickness and the feeling of tightness as you wear the clothes that used to fit you perfectly. It is thought that 75% of women experience morning sickness, so if you haven't at this point, then you can consider yourself lucky.

When you are expecting, it is thought that eating fruit not only provides you with essential nutrients that you need, but it can also be easy to eat for those times when you are feeling queasy. It can also keep your bathroom schedule regular. There is nothing worse than being pregnant, which already leads you to feel bloated, while also being constipated. A general rule of thumb to follow when it comes to eating fruit is the brighter, the better. This applies to vegetables as well. If the inside of the fruit or vegetable is particularly bright, this is a good indication that it contains a lot of nutrients.

Being fatigued is also pretty normal during your second month of pregnancy. Since your body is going through so many changes, it can be hard to adjust to this new lifestyle. You might find yourself getting tired more easily and needing more sleep throughout the day. Let your partner and your friends help you! Many pregnant women know that they are still capable of doing everything that they used to do before the pregnancy, but that doesn't mean that a little bit of help won't go a long way. Though you don't look very pregnant, your inner-body is still going through a lot. Do away with the heavy lifting and walking back and forth. Accept the help if it is offered.

You might notice an increase in vaginal discharge; this is normal, and it is happening due to the estrogen. Leukorrhea is a substance that is thin and milky. Your body produces it naturally when it is producing more estrogen.

This happens because the estrogen increases blood flow to the pelvic region, and this stimulates your body's mucous membranes. Leukorrhea actually serves a purpose other than making you wash more laundry. It helps by keeping the birth canal area primed and free of infections. Leukorrhea contains a healthy type of bacteria, so don't worry about cleaning it up or washing it away. Just let it do its job. When you do wash your vagina, make sure that you aren't using any soaps that are heavily scented or filled with chemicals. This can cause an imbalance in the healthy bacteria of your vagina.

The Third Month

As big as a lime now, your baby is busy making white blood cells in order to fight off germs that are around them. In the last month, your baby's intestines were developing and becoming entangled with the umbilical cord space, but now they are migrating back into your baby's abdominal area. The pituitary gland is now developing at the base of your baby's brain. This means that hormones are now being produced, allowing them to have children of their own one day. It is fascinating to think that this stage happens when your baby is only in its third month of development.

Much bigger than last month, your baby can be around 2-2 ¼ inches in size now. They will weigh about half an ounce. This is a dramatic jump in size, so you can tell that your baby has done a lot of growing from month two to month three. During this week, a milestone occurs. This is when your baby's digestive system becomes fully operational. Most of their systems are now fully formed, so this means that your little one will now experience contractions as their muscles flex due to their fetal digestive system.

Of course, there is still plenty of time for growth and maturing, but the digestive system is obviously going to be a system that is very important for once your baby is born. Your little one will need to know what to do with food after you give birth and begin feeding them. As your baby is practicing these contractions and movements, this primes the body for the task of eventually digesting food on its own one day. These contractions allow for food to pass through the digestive tract. It is likely at this check-up that you will finally be able to hear your baby's heartbeat! It is an emotional and exciting time for all mothers. Hearing the sound of your baby's heart, still beating very rapidly, will often speed up your own heart rate.

Your Changes

You are in the last month of your first trimester, a milestone for the expecting mother! At this point, your uterus is still about the size of a large grapefruit. It will begin to migrate from the bottom of your pelvis to the center of your abdomen. This is why many women begin showing at this stage in the pregnancy. After this happens, you will likely experience the relief of the constant pressure on your bladder. Prior to your uterus migrating, all of that pressure was being placed directly on your bladder, causing you to feel the urge to urinate all the time. With this new arrangement in your body, you shouldn't feel the need to go as frequently.

Your baby bump may or may not be showing by now. It can differ depending on the size of the baby and the woman. Remember, all pregnancies are unique. Whether you are showing a little, a lot, or not at all, you are still carrying the great responsibility of growing a tiny human being inside of you. Your clothes should definitely begin to feel even tighter now. Instead of wearing your usual jeans and shirts, you might want to invest in some maternity clothing or at least clothing that is more loose-fitting. Many women like to buy normal clothing during this stage, simply sizing up. Do whatever you need to do to stay comfortable.

A new symptom might have found its way to you, and that is dizziness. A lot of pregnant women in their third-month report having dizzy spells. Progesterone is thought to be the cause of this. Since your blood vessels are relaxing and widening during your pregnancy, your baby is able to receive more blood flow. If you think about it, you are literally being drained and depleted on a daily basis. So make sure that you are staying hydrated. Drinking enough fluids is essential to avoiding these dizzy spells, or worse, fainting spells.

Your blood pressure might be a little bit lower, and some women can also experience dizziness from having low blood sugar. This can happen if you are not eating regularly, which only has one thing to blame--nausea. Even if you do not feel like eating, you need to keep yourself regularly nourished somehow. Try to opt for things that are plain and free of strong smells. This will keep you from feeling sick when you try to eat. As mentioned, fruit can be easy for a lot of pregnant women to eat, and fruit also provides plenty of nutrients per serving. If you do encounter a dizzy spell despite your efforts to eat a balanced diet, lie down or sit down with your head lowered between your knees. Take a few deep breaths as you loosen any tight clothing you might be wearing. This feeling of being constricted can add to your dizzy spells. Once you feel well enough to stand up again, try to eat a small snack and drink plenty of water.

While sex might be the last thing on your mind while you are pregnant, there are different levels of sexual desire that you can experience during these next few months. During the third month, a lot of women report that they feel as though their sex drive is low. Since you are feeling so bloated, and often so sick, it makes sense that you do not feel like having a lot of sex during this time. The hormones will also impact your desire or lack of desire to have sex. Most women agree that they are just not in the mood during their third month of pregnancy, while a small percentage actually state that their desire has increased.

Chapter 2: The Second Trimester (4-6 Months)

Once you reach your second trimester, you have likely experienced most of the pregnancy symptoms that you can expect from now on. As your belly continues to grow, your baby continues to develop even more rapidly than before. Many milestones are reached during this portion of your pregnancy, including the gender reveal (if you choose to find out)! It can be one of the most exciting parts of your pregnancy, other than the actual moment that you go into labor. This chapter will cover what you can expect as you navigate through your second trimester of pregnancy.

The Fourth Month

Your baby's eyes have now begun experiencing movement. These small, side-to-side movements can be triggered by light. Even though their eyes are still closed, and will remain closed for a while, they can still often perceive light. As you probably know, a lot of babies develop a thumb-sucking habit. What you likely didn't know is that this habit can start during the fourth month of pregnancy. Though it is still fairly early on in the developmental stages, your baby might have that thumb-sucking instinct while still in the womb. Though they cannot exactly begin sucking their thumbs just yet, they are able to make sucking motions.

About the size of an avocado now, your baby has grown tremendously since the prior month. With a range of about 4-5 inches in length, they can weigh around 3-4 ounces. Their tiny backbone is gaining some strength as their muscles continue to develop. At this point, your baby can straighten out their neck if they want to. Not only are these muscles getting stronger, but their facial muscles are also getting stronger by the day. Your baby can now make certain facial expressions, such as squinting and frowning. Through their eyes are still closed, you can imagine that your baby is still making these faces as they experience certain things inside the womb.

As your baby's face continues to develop and appear more human, their skin is still translucent. If you were able to see your baby, you would be able to see through their skin and take a look at their blood vessels that are just underneath. Because there is no baby fat yet, the skin remains translucent until this fat develops and creates pigment. Your baby won't be this way for long, though. In a few weeks' time, their skin is going to become thicker and less translucent.

Your baby now has tiny bones in their ears, which means that they can actually hear your voice. Though it might not be clear as to what they are hearing, talk to your baby often. They will get used to the sound of your voice, and by the time they are born, your voice will be one that is recognizable and familiar to your baby. A lot of expecting mothers start reading to their children during this stage of pregnancy. Whether or not your baby can hear you properly, it is still great to use your voice as much as you can and talk to your baby frequently.

Your Changes

Your uterus is now growing at around the same pace as your fetus—this is very fast! If you were ever trying to hide the fact that you are pregnant, it is likely going to be very hard for you to do so in the fourth month. Your belly should be showing by now, and this means that all of your clothing is going to fit differently. This part of your pregnancy should feel relatively calm when you compare it to your first trimester. The second trimester tends to be filled with less nausea, which comes as a big relief for all expecting mothers.

During this time, you will notice that you are gaining weight rapidly. A lot of women can find this difficult, even while knowing that it is because a baby is growing and developing inside of their womb. Know that as long as you are eating properly, all of the weight you are gaining is necessary in order to keep your baby healthy and developing properly. Try to avoid junk food, even if your cravings are telling you otherwise. A little bit of indulgence every once in a while is okay, but you should be focused on eating more nutritious foods instead.

As your stomach continues to swell, you might find it surprising when your nose begins to swell too. Your pregnancy hormones can cause a great deal of nasal congestion, and unfortunately, this is one of those symptoms that can just continue to get worse as your pregnancy goes on. For some relief, you can safely try to use saline solution or nasal strips. Having a humidifier in your room is also thought to be helpful to ease your breathing.

The moment that most are waiting for—you get to find out if you are having a boy or a girl. Getting your ultrasound photos is a big milestone, and even if you do not wish to reveal the gender just yet, these are your first photos of your little one that you will get to treasure forever. While you can remain grateful for this moment, it is likely going to be the best feeling that you will experience in your fourth month. As your belly grows, your breasts are also going to be growing. This happens because of the hormones telling them that a baby is on the way. Your breasts might begin producing milk relatively early on during your pregnancy, anxiously anticipating the baby's arrival.

In prior months, you have likely experienced some constipation or bathroom trouble. This might increase for a whole new reason during your fourth month of pregnancy. While hormones were to blame earlier, your expanding uterus is now another reason for why you might not be able to regularly make a bowel movement. To keep things running smoothly, try to increase the amount of liquid that you are drinking. The more liquid you drink, the better chance you have of being able to use the bathroom.

Naturally, a bigger belly means more weight for you to carry. This can begin to impact your back. During your early months of pregnancy, your belly likely wasn't big enough to cause much strain, but this can all change in your fourth month. Try getting a prenatal massage to ease the pain, or have your partner rub your back at night. Make sure that you are staying off your feet as much as you can because this can also help alleviate some of the pain you are feeling.

The Fifth Month

Your little one is moving their hands a lot this month. As mentioned, they might even be sucking their thumb by now! Aside from this, it is common for your baby's hands to drift to their face and start to feel around. If you have yet to feel any movement, this month should be a lot different for you. Your baby is now likely squirming and moving around a lot more, possibly even kicking and punching. While it can be a funny feeling, it is a reassuring action that shows you that your baby is developing in a healthy way. You can sometimes see this movement from the outside of your belly, little feet or fists pushing forward.

At this point, you will likely already know if you are having a boy or a girl (if you have opted to receive this information). Many parents enjoy doing gender reveal parties. This becomes possible by your doctor writing down the gender on a piece of paper. You can get very creative if you wish to have your own gender reveal party. The paper with the gender is then given to a bakery or party shop to make a cake or balloons with either pink or blue coloration inside. There are many other ways to announce the gender, but today, lots of parents enjoy hosting this event because it is also a surprise to them.

If you are carrying a girl, her uterus is fully formed at this point. She has a vaginal canal that is already starting to develop and she even has some primitive eggs forming in her tiny ovaries. For a little boy, his testicles are about to descend. Right now, they are still growing in his abdomen. Once the scrotum is finished developing, then the testicles will drop. This can all happen within a few week's time.

Your baby has grown a lot by now! They can weigh a whopping 10 ounces, a big jump from the month earlier. About the size of a sweet potato, they can measure around 6-7 inches in length. Naturally, this is why you are able to feel their movements a lot more in the fifth month.

But your womb still has plenty of growing to do in order to accommodate your growing baby. Since there is still wiggle room, so to speak, your baby recognizes this and takes advantage of it frequently.

Your Changes

You are at the halfway point of your pregnancy! Believe it or not, there is not that much longer to go until you finally get to meet your little one in person. All of the symptoms that you are feeling now, especially the baby kicking, can make everything seem so much more real. A lot of mothers agree that, after this point, the time seems to fly by. Enjoy being pregnant while you can, even despite any challenging days that you might have. These little moments are unforgettable and one-of-a-kind. No matter how big or small your belly is, there is no doubt that you have a fast-developing baby inside.

At this point, your appetite has likely returned in full swing. Since nausea has likely subsided, you should feel ready and willing to eat just about anything. This can be a time when the intense cravings take over. While it is great to indulge in these cravings, you must make sure that you are also doing your best to keep a balanced diet. Also, don't forget to take your prenatal vitamin every day! It helps to keep track of what you eat each day. What would normally sustain you before you got pregnant is no longer going to be enough now that you are feeding two.

Your current wardrobe is likely stashed away and being replaced by loose-fitting clothing. Whether you have decided to buy a whole wardrobe of maternity clothing or simply size up from what you normally wear, you should be wearing things that allow you to feel comfortable and free of pressure. All pants should be pull-on, both for ease of access and your own personal comfort. Flowy dresses are also a great option for a woman in her fifth month of pregnancy. Invest in some comfortable shoes, as well. If your feet get swollen, wearing shoes that are tight can cause you aches and pains.

If you notice that your nails are stronger and your hair is healthier than ever, you can thank those pregnancy hormones. This happens because the hormones trigger a surge of circulation that is felt throughout your entire body. Extra nutrients are then distributed to the cells. Don't get too attached to these benefits, though, because your hair and nails will likely return to normal after delivery. A lot of women love this part of being pregnant. It is a chance to feel great about yourself when you are mainly feeling bloated and immobile.

You might be experiencing some heartburn or indigestion; this is normal. If this happens to you frequently after eating, try chewing a piece of sugarless gum after each meal. This will increase your saliva production which will then neutralize your gastric acids. It also helps to get those fluids back into your stomach where they are needed. Headaches are also a common symptom at this stage in your pregnancy. These headaches are typically triggered by hot conditions. If you are in a room that is overheated or too stuffy, you might just need to step out for some fresh air to avoid getting a headache. Dress in layers if you need to. This will allow you to avoid overheating if you do not have the option to step outside. Beware of the dizzy spells, as well. Unfortunately, they can still pop up when you least expect them.

The Sixth Month

You now have a pomegranate-sized baby! This little one is not so little anymore, measuring at almost 12 inches. At this point, they can weigh over 1 pound. Your baby is putting on weight, and this is a great sign of healthy development. This means that fat and muscle are continuing to develop, both essential to becoming a healthy newborn. There is also additional weight because of their growing organs and bones. Each week, they keep getting bigger to fit the size of your baby's body. If you were able to see your baby right now, there is a good chance you'd know what they would look like. Their tiny face is nearly fully formed, and they have eyelashes, eyebrows, and hair. However, the hair is still free of pigment, so it would appear white. Their skin is still fairly see-through, but that won't be the case for much longer.

Many sounds can be heard by your baby now. Make sure that you are still talking to them, reading to them, and singing to them when you can. Not only is your voice a lot clearer to them, but they can also hear the sound of your lungs breathing, your heart beating, and even sounds that you pass by on the street. It is important that you and your partner both keep talking to your baby so that they will be familiar with your voices by the time you deliver. This is one way that you can start bonding even before the baby is born.

Since your baby is even bigger now, your belly button has likely been pushed forward to become an outie. Whether you started with an innie or an outie, it is common for most pregnant women to temporarily have an outie during this point in the pregnancy due to the baby's growth. Your swelling uterus is what causes this to happen. After you give birth, your belly button will go back to what it looked like before. You might also notice some stretch marks forming, not only on your belly but on your thighs too. So many pregnant women go through this, and you can think about them as your badges of honor. Your body is literally changing in order to bring life into this world, so know that it is doing its best. Rubbing shea butter on your stretch marks can help to fade them if they start to bother you.

As the weeks' progress, you should feel your baby lower and lower in your abdomen. Do not confuse this with the final "drop," though. Your baby will eventually drop before you go into labor. The feeling of your baby getting lower is simply happening because of the growth that is taking place inside of your uterus. This is when you are going to be extra thankful for clothing that does not push on your belly. While it might not be painful, it can become uncomfortable, especially if you need to be sitting down for long periods of time.

Your Changes

A unique pregnancy symptom you might be experiencing at this point is carpal tunnel syndrome. It is normal to have a feeling of numbness in your wrists and fingers, even if you aren't using them more than you usually do. While repetitive motion can contribute to this symptom, it is typically triggered by the swelling that you experience while pregnant. Fluids can tend to accumulate in your lower body, therefore not reaching your upper body as much as they used to. You can feel some relief from the carpal tunnel by avoiding sleeping on your hands or using your arms to prop your pillow up. Nighttime is a way for your body to reset the circulation because you will be lying down. It can also help to just shake everything out every so often. If you do work in some kind of an office setting that requires typing or writing, take breaks frequently.

Another unique symptom that you might experience is red and itchy palms. This one also has little to do with the activities that you participate in throughout the day. Much like all of the other pregnancy symptoms, you can blame your hormones for this one, as well. This is a fairly mundane symptom, but it is one that you should definitely keep an eye on. In rare cases, it can be an indication of a pregnancy complication known as cholestasis of pregnancy. This is more common in the third trimester, but you shouldn't rule anything out. If your palms start to bother you to the point where you are in constant pain, or if you notice that the symptoms just won't go away, contact your doctor for a consultation.

There are a plethora of other random symptoms that you might be feeling, too. The sixth month tends to be one where the most obscure symptoms will pop up, sometimes surprising you. Your mouth might be producing additional saliva, and you might also notice a metallic taste. Skin tags (small, soft skin growths) can appear out of nowhere, and your vision might even temporarily change. These are all normal symptoms that must be dealt with during pregnancy, but know that they won't last forever. The best way to get relief is simply by taking it easy. While you might be an energetic person by nature, try not to do too much. Even if you feel up to it at the moment, your body will face repercussions in the future.

Constipation can become an issue again. You should be very keen on dealing with it by now. As stated before, you need to keep drinking plenty of water to keep everything in your digestive system moving. This is the easiest and best thing that you can do for yourself if you are feeling constipated all the time. Drinking prune juice can also help because it will soften your stool. While taking actual laxatives isn't typically recommended, using nature's laxatives can work just as well.

Chapter 3: The Third Trimester (7-9 Months)

You are in the final stretch, quite literally! Your pregnancy is nearing its end, and for some women, delivery does come early. While you are feeling your baby gets even bigger and watching yourself grow, a lot of planning happens in the third trimester. From making a birth plan to decorating the nursery, you are going to be pretty busy. It is usually in the third trimester that a lot of women decide to have a baby shower. Of course, that is a personal decision, but it is a fun way to celebrate with your loved ones a final time before the baby arrives.

The Seventh Month

You are carrying a baby that is roughly the size of an entire head of lettuce now. At 15 inches long and over 2 pounds, you should be feeling your baby a lot during the seventh month. Your baby can now experience REM (rapid eye movement) sleep. This means that your baby is likely having dreams! It is exciting to think about what they might be dreaming about while they are waiting to come into this world. Brain wave activity has been measured in studies showing that your baby actually does go through different cycles of sleep. These are the same cycles that you go through when you are sleeping.

Before this point, their eyes have been closed while they were developing. Now, they are able to open their eyes and blink. The eyelashes are fully formed, as well. Before, your baby could squint and frown. Now, there is a chance that they are sticking their tongue out on a regular basis. Many doctors can't explain why babies do this in the womb, but it is likely because they can now feel that they have a tongue that has developed. They also might be tasting the amniotic fluid.

Your baby is dropping lower now, getting into a position that will be suitable for birth. If all is going as planned, their head should begin moving downward. This process can happen at different rates for different women. Some babies never get into the "correct" position, but this does not mean that a natural birth isn't possible. You can deliver feet-first, and there is also the option of having a C-section. Know that while you are making your birth plan, so much can change once you go into labor. Make sure that you are willing to be flexible with the plan because you might have no choice once your baby is ready to come out.

Aside from blinking and making faces, your baby is now also likely sucking a lot more. They can also get the hiccups! This can be felt by you, and it is adorable, to say the least. This is also a time when your baby is going to practice taking deeper breaths, preparing for what breathing will be like in the outside world. They know exactly what they need to do in order to prepare for delivery, just as your body seems to know exactly what to do.

While you might be feeling more uncomfortable as your size is increasing, so is your baby. The space that your baby calls home is not growing as much as it used to in the past. This is why they might be moving around a lot more, eager to explore. All of the kicking, punching, and squirming can be attributed to curiosity. Your baby wants to see exactly how much room they have to move around inside of the womb.

Your Changes

In the seventh month, you have probably experienced your fair share of sciatica. This is what is known as the tingling leg pain that you feel. This is the kind of symptom that might keep you up at night because it prohibits you from fully relaxing. Your feet can also get swollen, and your back might be aching more than usual. While you are noticing these symptoms all day and all night, they can often feel more intense at night when your body needs to relax. A lot of this discomfort comes from the fact that your baby is now so big that they might be putting pressure on your sciatic nerve. This is located in the lower part of your spine.

Another symptom of the position that your baby is currently in can be shooting, sharp pain that stems from the sciatic nerve. It can be felt from your butt, all the way down the backs of your legs. This is a more intense version of sciatica that many pregnant women do experience. Relief is hard to find for this symptom, but if your baby shifts positions, this can take some of the pressure off of your nerve and temporarily relieve you of the discomfort. Otherwise, try to stay off your feet as much as possible. In order to remedy most other symptoms, proper rest and relaxation are what you will need to make your sciatica feel better too.

You might find that your skin is more sensitive than usual. Even if you have never experienced sensitive skin before, your pregnancy can tend to bring this out. Some parts of your body might become easily irritated, red, itchy, and dry. Make sure that you are moisturizing daily with a fragrance-free moisturizer that was designed for sensitive skin. This will keep your skin calm and will keep you free of pain. Your most sensitive spot is naturally going to be the skin on your belly. Because, of all the stretching that it is doing, this skin can become irritated very easily. Certain fabrics might even trigger the irritation. Make sure that your clothing is made of breathable material.

Bloating and gas are common symptoms that you will continue to experience as you progress into your third trimester. Your uterus is putting pressure on your rectum, and you might not be able to help it when that gas must be released. Your sluggish digestive system is also playing a role in the amount of bloating and gas that you are experiencing. Though you might have a perfectly fine appetite, try to change the way you eat your meals. Instead of having 3 large meals, break this up into 6 small ones that you can eat throughout the day. This will make it easier on your digestive system, and it can help you feel full longer. The same rule still applies—eat a balanced diet.

The Eighth Month

You are now carrying a child that is comparable to the size of a cantaloupe. At 16-17 inches long and about 3-4 pounds, your baby is almost fully developed! At this point, your baby's major organs are all fully formed except for the lungs. Since your baby is still inhaling amniotic fluid, their lungs are still in a practice stage. Once they are born, they will learn how to transition to breathing air. If you were to deliver your baby this week, chances are that you would give birth to a baby who is healthy and ready to take on the world. As mentioned, some women do go into labor early, so be ready! The baby's skin is no longer translucent, as a pigment has now surfaced. You would be able to see a very clear image of what your baby is going to look like if you were able to look inside the womb.

Your baby has been practicing a lot of things in the last few weeks. They know that it is almost time to meet you and enter the world. Swallowing more frequently and breathing deeply are just two of the functions they have practiced lately. Your baby's digestive system is now fully ready to begin working once they are born. In anticipation of the birth, you can expect your baby to be very active at this point. There will be plenty of kicking and squirming for you to feel. These are your last few weeks of pregnancy, so enjoy them and the feelings that they bring.

Most babies have settled into their birthing position by now. This is a curled position, known as fetal position, with the head down and bottom-up. Your baby will fit better through the birth canal if they are able to get into this position, but sometimes this does not happen. As mentioned, it is okay if your baby is in a breech position (feet down, head up). 5% of babies do end up in this position. There is still time for them to flip over before delivery, but if that does not change, then your doctor will tell you what your best options are for having the easiest delivery possible.

Since sleep cycles have been discovered, your baby should be sleeping at regular intervals now. They probably have a sleep schedule that mirrors your own. This means, if you are up and active, the baby is likely going to be awake. Once you go to sleep, this should calm them down. This is an ideal cycle, but it doesn't always end up syncing up perfectly. There are still many nights when your baby will likely keep you awake because they just aren't ready to go to sleep yet. There isn't much you can do to change this, but it will give you insight into how great a sleeper your baby may or may not be after they are born.

Your Changes

In preparation for delivery, your body might be sending you some signals that are known as Braxton Hicks contractions. This occurs when you feel your uterus tightening, but what differentiates them from labor contractions is that they are just practicing for when your water actually breaks and you begin to experience regular contractions. If there isn't a pattern to the contractions, and if they aren't lasting for a very long time, then they are likely just Braxton Hicks contractions. They typically last 15-30 seconds, but some women have reported them lasting for up to 2 minutes. Another way to tell them apart from true labor contractions is by moving around. If you change positions, the Braxton Hicks contractions will likely stop or at least lessen in severity.

Since there is so much additional weight for your body to carry, you are likely going to experience an increase in leg cramping/spasming, especially right before bedtime. This can happen in your calves, and doctors aren't sure about exactly what causes the sensation. The most likely cause is simply the sudden shift from your legs holding all of that additional weight to now lying down and attempting to redistribute the way that it carries the weight. With the permission of your doctor, you might need to incorporate more calcium or magnesium into your daily vitamin routine to help your legs feel better.

It is something that isn't frequently discussed, but yes, pregnant women often get hemorrhoids. These are actually varicose veins in the rectum that are swollen, and they can be very uncomfortable. If you are in pain when you sit down, you might need to rely on some ice packs to help relieve the urge to keep shifting in your seat. Warm baths can also help if you are at home and experiencing hemorrhoids. Another option is the use of witch hazel to soothe the pain. It is a great and natural solution that can be applied directly to your anus. Though it might be embarrassing to experience such a problem, know that this is all a normal part of your pregnancy. This is an indication that your baby is growing big and strong, so your body must make quick adjustments in order to accommodate this.

Your breasts are likely bigger than they have ever been by this point. You might experience colostrum, which is a term that indicates leaky breasts. Colostrum is a yellowish fluid that is sort of like the precursor to breast milk. While there is nothing that you can do to stop the leaking, you can wear breast pads inside your bra to create a buffer for the leak. This is also a very normal part of being into your third trimester, and you can think about it in a positive way knowing that, if you decide to breastfeed, these are the very first nutrients your baby will receive after being born.

The Ninth Month

You are officially in your last month of pregnancy! Your baby is as large as a bundle of kale by now, likely weighing around 6 pounds or more. They are about 18-19 inches in length. During these last few weeks, your baby's hearing is going to be incredibly sharp. From hearing your voice to the music you play, your baby is definitely going to be listening closely. Another big change that happens sometime during the ninth month is the "drop." This is when your baby shifts positions, moving downward toward your pelvis. This is an indication that your little one is almost ready to come out into the world.

This is finally a point where your baby is going to slow down on growth and development. All of the development that has happened in the womb has led you to this stage in your pregnancy. Most of the rest of it will take place after the baby is born. However, during this time, your baby's bones are still not quite fused together yet. This is normal, and this is going to assist with your baby's head maneuvering through the birth canal during delivery. During the first few years of your baby's life, their bones will become harder and stronger.

Most of your baby's systems have reached their final stage of maturity, as they are done with their in-womb development. The only system that needs to catch up once your baby is born is the digestive system. This one takes longer because your baby is used to being fed directly through the umbilical cord. After birth, your baby will either be drinking your breastmilk or formula and given the chance to learn how to digest and process food on their own. A fully functional digestive system can take up to 1-2 years to mature. This is why your baby is still going to be spitting up after feeding for a while, but don't worry, this is all perfectly normal when it comes to the behaviors of a newborn.

There is no doubt about it, your baby looks like an infant in this final stage. They will have skin that has a slight pink tinge to it with chubby arms and legs. Their tiny facial features are fully formed, giving you a glimpse at a part of yourself and a part of your partner. All of their fingers and toes should have separated, and their little heart is working effectively. Your baby is now a tiny human, and it is only a matter of time before you finally get to meet one another.

Your Changes

Your back is likely going to be aching more than ever in these final weeks—it's normal. Since your baby is basically fully grown, this is a lot of extra weight for you to carry around as you try to remain mobile in your last few moments of pregnancy. Your walk has likely turned into a waddle because your baby has dropped. There is nothing wrong with this walk, as it is actually normal for your body to adopt a new method since the connective tissue in your body is softening in preparation for your delivery. Embrace your walk, and know that you have a healthy baby to look forward to meeting very soon.

While your joint flexibility has increased more than ever, there also comes a downside. You are likely experiencing a lot more pelvic pain than usual. Since your baby's head is lower in your pelvis than ever before and your uterus is as heavy as can be, this will cause the soreness that you feel. When you walk around, you are likely to feel it more. It is a good idea to stay off your feet as much as possible in these last few weeks. Though it can be tempting to walk around because walking can often induce labor, you need to be smart about how much time you are actually spending on your feet.

If you do not feel that your baby has dropped, this isn't a bad thing. Some babies actually do not drop before labor. Though most will drop within the ninth month of pregnancy, some babies stay in the same position until it is finally time for delivery. If your baby is insistent on staying put, then you are likely to feel pressure on your uterus. It might be uncomfortable for you to enjoy a meal, even if you are starving. This pressure can make it feel like there is no more room for food inside your stomach, even though there really is enough room.

Ironically, you will feel your baby moving around less during this final month of pregnancy. This happens because their space to move around is now limited because of how big they are. Instead of kicking and jabbing, you might only be able to feel squirming. You are also going to experience a lot of gas and burping during this time, and you will find that it feels so good to let it all out. When you eat, try not to eat too quickly. This will push more air into your body, therefore creating more gas for you to have to pass.

Heartburn and indigestion should also be familiar to you in the ninth month. Your stomach is getting pushed around by your uterus, as mentioned, so you might not be able to eat as much as your appetite feels like you can handle. Try eating smaller meals so that you can still enjoy your food without too much trouble digesting it. Remember, all of this pressure will soon be gone once you give birth to your little one.

Part 2: Baby's First Year—Milestones and Mental Leaps

In this part of the guide, you are going to learn everything that you need to know regarding your newborn baby. From feedings to first steps, you are going to experience all of these joys with your little one. You will find that they are going to look up to you, so you need to remember that you are their main role model in life. Behavior is mirrored at this age, so to ensure that your baby is learning as much as possible, you need to lead by example. As your infant gets closer to becoming a toddler, there are many milestones to look forward to that will be sure to delight and surprise you.

Chapter 4: 1st Month-3rd Month

Congratulations! You now have a bundle of joy in your life that you have worked so hard to carry for the past 9 months. In the first 3 months of your baby's life, so many changes will happen developmentally. Not only are you getting to know your little one's personality, but you will also be able to see them accomplish many milestones and allow your heart to swell with pride as you do. From what you can expect to what is about to happen next, this is a very exciting time for both the baby and the parents. It is a fast-paced period of growth and discovery.

First Month

Milestones

Achieved Milestones

- Eye-tracking

- Gripping an object placed into the hand
- Notices faces and people within close range
- Making throaty noises
- Crying subsides when held by a caregiver
- Has reflexes
- Stops crying to notice a sound/voice
- Moving limbs in symmetry
- Can recognize mother's breast

Emerging Milestones

- Eye-tracking from side to side
- Attempts to swipe or hit objects
- Noticing hands and legs
- Ability to briefly hold objects
- Making cooing sounds
- Crying subsides at sight of caregiver
- Can lift head slightly during tummy time
- Will respond to caregiver's voice with cooing and throaty sounds
- Will learn that hands and legs are bodily extensions

- Knows the difference between a mother's breast and bottle

Development

Cognitive: By one month of age, your baby should be expecting regular feedings. This means that, if not fed during certain intervals of time, you will notice additional fussing or crying. Your baby will be able to look at and acknowledge people, either by simply using their eyes or potentially making noises when they notice someone new enters the room. They will be able to tell the difference between a soft item and a hard item; textures will likely be very interesting to them. If you eat something that changes the taste of your breast milk, your baby will have a reaction to this. If you notice a puckered expression or a refusal to eat, this might be an indication that your one-month-old is telling you that the taste of the milk has changed.

Physical: Though the movements will remain jerky for a little while, your baby should be thrusting their arms and legs. While this is an exploration, it also serves as a way to strengthen the muscles. You will also notice more symmetrical limb movement from your little one. As they figure out that certain limbs are parts of their own body, you will start to see this symmetrical movement. Your baby might also be putting their hand into their mouth a lot. After this discovery, a lot of babies will even begin gnawing on their tiny fingers or fist. Since they still cannot hold their head up on their own, it will fall backward if unsupported. Make sure that you are holding your baby with proper neck support at all times.

Social/Emotional: Since your baby cannot talk yet, crying is the main form of communication. If they are content, they will happily stay in a certain spot or position. When they need something, however, the crying will begin. There are different cries for different reasons. For example, a cry for hunger might sound different than a cry for a dirty diaper. As your baby learns to recognize the faces they see around them, they will also be able to provide eye contact. This helps them with their focus, but it is also a way for them to connect with the individual in front of them. Your baby is going to be very eager for these connections at this age. This is great because they will likely be meeting a lot of new people in their first month of life!

Is Your Baby Healthy?

Your baby is likely to weigh around 9 pounds, on average. Since birth, it is normal for an infant to gain around 1½-2 lbs. In terms of length, you should also see a difference here. Most babies grow around 1½-2 inches, as well. Know that these are just the average estimates, and if your baby is not growing exactly as indicated, this does not necessarily mean that they are unhealthy. During your first check-up with the doctor, official measurements will be taken. These will be compared to the ones taken at birth, and then your doctor will be able to refer to a growth chart.

Pay attention to the way your baby's senses are working. Do they respond to loud noises? Look at bright lights or colors? Can they recognize the sound of your voice and the feeling when you hold them? This, along with regular feeding, is how you can form an indication of your baby's health from home. As long as you notice normal development and your baby is willing to eat, then it should all be going pretty well. Of course, your first doctor's visit will be able to provide you with more concrete insight as to what your baby is actually experiencing and how they are developing.

Keep an eye on your baby's eyes, nose, and ears. They can all provide you with hints that something might be wrong, depending on how they look. If your baby's eyes appear glassy or bloodshot, along with a stuffy nose, they might have developed a cold. Their ears also might feel tender to the touch, indicating a possible ear infection. Babies have very fragile immune systems, so if you notice these symptoms, it is a good idea to get to the doctor right away. While adults can typically heal on their own from a common cold, it can feel a lot more severe to a newborn baby.

Even if you cannot see any external symptoms, yet your baby won't stop crying no matter how hard you try to soothe them, it is also a good idea to take your baby to the doctor. There could be things happening internally that you wouldn't know about unless the doctor takes a look. Inconsolable crying, for whatever reason, should not last for hours at a time. Some babies are able to be soothed easier than others, but crying for hours at a time is a sign that a trip to the doctor might be necessary.

How To Help Development

The best way to help your baby's developmental progress is by creating a routine. This will allow your baby to feel comfortable and familiar as to what is going on each day. Stick to a feeding schedule that fits with your lifestyle. Do your best to create a sleep schedule, as well. It can be very hard for certain infants to regulate their sleeping schedules within the first month, but it is worth a try. Babies typically sleep for most of the day during their first month of life, and when nighttime comes, they are wide awake. This is why it is important that you create a schedule that you can alter. Keep your baby engaged and social during the day so that they are tired by the time it gets dark out.

Introduce your baby to as many new people as you can. This likely won't be very hard, as a lot of people will probably be dying to meet your little one anyway. Your baby is going to know yourself and your partner as their primary caregivers, but it is great for their social development to meet and be handled by other people. This can be confusing or interesting to your baby and don't be surprised if they immediately burst out in tears after leaving mommy's arms. Babies attach very quickly, but there are certain levels of attachment that are healthy, as well as levels that can become unhealthy. You will want to build your trust with your baby, showing them that they will return to you, even after being held by a new person.

Talk to your baby using real words and sentences. While it can be tempting to coo at your little one, it is actually going to help their development more if they hear you speaking properly. This is how they are going to make sense of language and communication. If you start talking to them from a very young age, they will also be more likely to begin mimicking the sounds that you make. This is the first stage of being able to speak and communicate effectively. Your baby will likely be fascinated as you talk to them in your native tongue, unable to take their eyes off you.

Second Month

Milestones

Achieved Milestones:

- Can raise head 45 degrees during tummy time
- Holds head straight when sitting in a supported position
- Can support partial weight on elbows
- Virtually follows objects in an arc formation
- Searches for sounds by turning head
- Recognizes faces
- Coos and grunts
- Smiles at familiar people
- Becomes fussy when bored

Emerging Milestones:

- Ability to raise head 90 degrees during tummy time
- Raising the head and looking up while sitting in a supported position

- Can place complete weight on elbows and forearms
- Follows objects within 180 degrees of their line of sight
- Recognizes faces, voices, and objects
- Squealing and babbling
- Smiling spontaneously at people
- Trying to imitate voices and tones

Development

Cognitive: Your baby will now be paying close attention to the faces that they see. Instead of staring at a face as though they are in a haze, they are tracking individual details of each face in front of them. Your baby will now have better coordination between hearing and brain function. They are going to look for the sound by turning their head in order to determine where the noise is coming from. As mentioned, different cries can determine different feelings. By now, you will know that your two-month-old has several cries that vary depending on what they want or need. There will be a hunger cry, a cry for when a diaper is soiled, a cry for when they are feeling antsy, and so on.

Physical: When you hold your baby up with support, their head should be able to stay straight fairly easily. These muscles develop very quickly for newborns, especially since they are so eager to look around at all there is to see and hear. You might also notice your baby trying to push up onto their elbows or forearms during tummy time. This is getting your baby one step closer to the scooting/crawling stage. Now, when your baby moves their limbs, the movements aren't as jerky as they used to be. The movements should appear smoother and more purposeful. Hand-eye coordination will also improve significantly. When your baby wants to grab something, they will likely be able to grab it on the first try if it is within reaching distance.

Social/Emotional: Smiling is the biggest milestone of the month. Your baby will likely be flashing many smiles at the sight of familiar or friendly faces. If you ask your baby questions, you will likely get a response in the form of gurgles or cooing. Self-soothing is something that you might also notice that your baby is doing. This can be anything from bringing their hands to their mouth while they are crying to sucking their thumb for comfort. Boredom also becomes something that your two-month-old can experience. This can cause them to become fussy or grumpy. This is actually another significant milestone because it shows you that your baby is developing unique emotions. They might be playing with a toy one minute and then throwing it on the ground and crying the next minute because they grew bored with the activity.

Is Your Baby Healthy?

There are a few signs that you can look for if you are concerned about your baby's developmental progress. One of the biggest signs to look for is if your baby cannot hold their head up, even despite pushing themselves up on their forearms during tummy time. The same level of concern is valid if your baby is struggling to keep their head straight while you are helping them sit in a supported position. Watch your baby's eyes. Do they respond to stimuli that are in front or to the side of them? Your baby should be moving their eyes a significant amount, and if they don't, this could indicate possible cognitive issues.

Most 2-month-olds will frequently put their hands in their mouths, as mentioned. This is both a self-soothing technique, as well as an exploration of their body. If your baby isn't bringing their hands up, this could be another indication that something is wrong or developing at a slower pace. A quiet baby can seem like a great thing, but a baby who never coos or smiles can be a cause for concern. In the first few months of your baby's life, their personality should be shining through. If you notice little response from your little one, it would be worth bringing it up with your doctor.

Of course, the best time to discuss any of your concerns is during your baby's two-month check-up. Even if you think the issue is minor, your doctor will be able to put you at ease and explain to you exactly how well your baby is developing. There are also certain screening tests that you will be offered to check for developmental disorders. Though they aren't mandatory, a lot of parents do opt for infant screening in order to catch any issues at an early stage. Listen to your maternal instinct. You are likely having these worries for a good reason, and remember, there is no such thing as asking too many questions when it comes to your baby's health and wellness.

How To Help Development

To help your baby continue on the right path, make sure to include plenty of tummy time in your daily routine. Not only does tummy time strengthen neck muscles so your baby can hold their head up on their own, but it actually strengthens muscles throughout the entire body. This is an ideal way to stimulate your baby's physical growth, according to pediatricians. You can have 3-5 sessions of tummy time daily, each lasting for around 5 minutes. Most babies really enjoy this time because it provides them with a new perspective and a feeling of independence. Don't forget to put some brightly colored toys in front of them on the ground for them to interact with.

Play with distance more. Encourage your baby to look for you from across the room by using your voice and waving your arms. This is an interactive game that is fun for an infant, and it also improves their cognitive ability to focus on things and to recognize things. You can begin to do this with toys, as well, showing your baby a brightly colored toy from afar and seeing if you can get a reaction. Experiment with different sounds. Your baby should be very reactive to high-pitched and low-pitched noises, along with the sound of your voice, which should be most comforting.

As your baby's social skills are developing daily, continue to let them meet with plenty of other people. It is likely that you are still going to be getting a lot of visitors who are eager to meet the little one. Try to get the whole family involved with playtime, showing your baby that it can be fun to interact in a group setting. This can often be very exciting for a two-month-old, and it will usually elicit a great response in return. Seeing so many people that your baby loves in one place is genuinely exciting. This is also a great way to improve your baby's memory. If they see family members in this setting daily, they will begin to remember their faces.

While you might want to jump for joy during every tiny milestone, know that this is only the beginning. You do need to allow your baby to explore and discover on their own. Providing positive reinforcement is a great thing, and you should continue providing it. Try not to guide your little one so much to the developmental stages that you feel they should be reaching. They will get there when the time is right, and they will know what they need to do to get there on their own when they are ready.

Third Month

Milestones

Achieved Milestones:

- Regularly lifts head to 45 degrees during tummy time
- Pushes legs down when held vertically
- Bringing hands to mouth
- Grasping objects that are close
- Shaking objects that are held
- Tracking moving objects/people
- Being quiet or reserved around strangers
- Strong back muscles from tummy time
- Can imitate certain actions
- Supports entire body weight on arms

Emerging Milestones:

- Moving head 90 degrees
- Bearing weight on feet when held on the ground
- Bringing hands together

- Attempts to grab objects beyond their reach
- Hitting an object to a surface during playtime
- Moving head to track objects/people all around
- Becoming anxious in the presence of strangers
- Rolling over in one direction

Development

Cognitive: When your baby sees you from across the room, they might express joy or excitement because they recognize that you are headed their way. If they hear something of interest, they will be able to turn their head in order to locate where the sound is coming from. This is an indication that your baby's brain is able to locate sources, which is a great sign. No matter if the sound causes joy, fear, or curiosity, your baby will likely still be interested in locating it. You should be able to have "conversations" with your baby now. Though they cannot respond with words, they will still respond with chortles, grunts, cooing, and more. You will also notice more imitation this month, with both sounds and actions.

Physical: You should feel that your baby's head is very steady during feeding and while being held in your arms. With all of the tummy time that your baby is having, this is causing their muscles to develop rapidly which is a great thing. A big physical milestone is the desire to stand when placed feet-first onto a surface. If your baby has this instinct already, then you can expect them to be walking sooner than you think. When your baby is on their back, you might notice that they are kicking and stretching more. This is an exploration of movement, and it is also a small milestone. Overall, your baby should be sleeping about an hour less than they did last month. The average infant sleeps for 16 hours, so you can expect your three-month-old to sleep around 15 hours.

Social/Emotional: Smiling is one of the most important social responses that your baby can have toward people. Since communication is limited, a smile is worth a thousand words. You might also hear your baby bust out in the giggles this month! Laughter is a beautiful sound, and your baby will become amused very easily. While your baby can be very friendly and bubbly toward familiar people, you might notice a reserved version of their personality when they are introduced to strangers. This shows that they are aware that the person is new. It is actually a good sign, and once you show your baby that this new person can be trusted, they will open up and start acting more bubbly again.

Is Your Baby Healthy?

Similar signs last month can also apply this month. As stated, a quiet baby is not necessarily a bad thing, but a baby who never laughs, smiles, or gurgles can be a cause for concern. Your baby should be making some noise every day aside from crying. If they still aren't doing that at this stage, mention the behavior to your doctor. This can be a serious sign of a developmental delay. Sometimes, this progress can be made up with the help of more interactive play and experiences. Other times, the delay is a sign of a learning disability.

If your baby's head is still bobbing back and forth seemingly uncontrollably, this is not a good sign. By the third month, your baby should have a very strong head, neck, and back muscles. Even despite tummy time, if your little one isn't able to control their head on their own, this could be an indication of some kind of physical developmental delay. Also, make sure that your baby can support their own head when you first pick them up. Though it is still necessary to assist them with a little bit of neck support, they should be able to maintain initial control over their head when being picked up.

Not being able to hold onto an object is another sign of a developmental delay in a three-month-old. By now, your baby should be holding onto objects, possibly even banging them on surfaces in front of them. If you notice that your baby cannot even grasp an object for a long period of time, mention this to your doctor. You will also need to pay attention to their grip. By now, your baby should be able to grip fairly hard. An abnormally loose grip can mean that there is a delay.

If an object or a person is moving within your baby's field of vision, no matter what is happening, your baby should be responsive to this either by looking or making a verbal response. When your baby simply does not react, then this is likely an indication that there is some kind of a developmental delay occurring. It is a good idea to keep a checklist to ensure that your baby is on track each month. You can reference it each month, looking at the progress that is being made.

How To Help Development

Interact with your baby as much as possible. It might seem silly, but explain what you are doing as you carry your baby around the house. You already know that hearing words and sentences being spoken can encourage learning and imitation, so make sure that you regularly narrate activities that you do together because you never know what your baby might understand, even from such a young age. Show them that you are listening to their responses, as well. If they respond to you or "talk" to you, it helps to show your baby that you will reply because this will prepare them for how to have an actual conversation.

Select activities that will promote tracking, like playing with toy cars that have the ability to move all-around your baby. You can also utilize toys that are placed on strings and have a wide range of mobility. These are the kind of activities that can make sure your baby is right on track with their tracking abilities. Use sounds to get your baby's attention. Making silly sounds should cause your baby to respond, and this can often be a fun game to play together. A three-month-old is going to have great listening ability, so it is up to you to get them to listen.

Along with these tips, also ensure that you are maintaining a regular schedule. This includes your feeding schedule, playtime, tummy time, socialization, and sleeping. In order to avoid developmental delays, having your baby on a routine shows them their first sense of regularity. If they are confused and wondering what is going to happen next each day, then they are less likely going to be developing and learning because their routine doesn't have enough structure to it. The self-discipline that it takes on your behalf is what will regulate your little one's schedule, and you will both feel thankful for it. Everyone is happier when they are able to get enough rest and have a sense of familiarity. If a baby's routine is disrupted, it is very easy to see the consequences. You will experience a lot more fussiness, and your baby will be expressing how they do not enjoy what is happening. Noticing a spike in fussy behavior could be an indication that a routine has been disrupted.

Chapter 5: 4th Month-6th Month

Your little one should now be as playful as ever. Each day, they are likely to surprise you by their willingness to explore and their curious mind. Being a parent to a baby who is under one year old can be filled with many different celebrations, as well as pitfalls. Your baby might not allow you to get any sleep at night, but that charming smile and adorable giggle are enough to make up for it. As your little one enters the second trimester of life, they will be babbling and, eventually, trying different solid foods to see which ones they enjoy most. Have fun during this time because your baby will give you many candid reactions that you will never forget.

Fourth Month

Milestones

Achieved Milestones:

- Responds to basic sounds and words
- Regularly supports the body with arms during tummy time
- Smiles and laughs while looking at faces
- Regularly tracks objects
- Can sit upright with support
- Makes basic movements during tummy time
- Holds toys with both hands
- Has different cries for different feelings
- Pays close attention to new faces and objects

Emerging Milestones:

- Will respond to their own name
- Rolls over from tummy onto the back
- Responds differently to different facial expressions

- Can track objects that are further away
- Can sit without support for short periods of time
- Crawls when placed on tummy
- Can pass toys from one hand to the other
- Makes different sounds for different feelings
- Supports weight on both legs while standing with support
- Shows curiosity when seeing new people and objects

Development

Cognitive: Your baby is starting to understand cause and effect. For example, when you put your baby into a feeding position, you will notice that their mouth automatically opens. Your little one also has a better memory now, remembering different people and objects that they might only see every once in a while. Understanding affection, your baby should be responsive to your hugs and kisses. This is especially true when the affection is given by the primary caregiver. Sadness is a feeling that your baby should regularly be expressing. When you leave the room, your baby might cry to show you that they are sad. This crying should subside as you return. Sadness isn't the only reason why your little one will cry. They will give you different tones for different feelings.

Physical: One of the biggest changes that you will notice is that your baby can now hold their head up on their own when they are in your arms! As you pick your baby up from a lying down position, their neck muscles should be strong enough to keep their head in place. Your baby has balance while in an assisted position. No more wobbling and falling over because your baby has strong lower back muscles, now. While speech isn't happening just yet, it is developing rapidly. Infants find it easy to say words with M, D, and B. You will typically notice their babbling beginning with these letters. Another big physical development is your baby's ability to roll over! Tummy time can be turned into tummy and back time.

Social/Emotional: Imitation should be happening frequently. From expressions to sounds, your baby will be very curious about other human behaviors. They will show a preference toward familiar people—for example, those that they see on a regular basis. This is an example of how your baby is telling you when they are comfortable. And strangers don't always elicit a shy response. Your baby might like to stare at a newcomer or try to get their attention by playing coy. Babies who are particularly social love meeting new people everywhere you go. This can make a standard trip to the grocery store extra long because of your baby's social tendencies. Don't be surprised if your baby actually starts crying when the new person approaches. This can be overwhelming for some.

Is Your Baby Healthy?

When your baby cannot move their eyes in a coordinated way by this point, this is abnormal. There might be a little bit of lag due to the ocular muscles still developing, but a response that takes longer than a few seconds might be a cause for concern. Much like last month, a lack of smiling at all means that there is likely something that is not connecting cognitively for your baby. This can also be a sign of social detachment, which can become a big problem if it is not addressed early on in your little one's life.

Having a wobbly neck by the fourth month is not normal, either. Because of all the tummy time and muscle formation, your baby should be lifting their head on their own regularly. If you notice any struggles, bring this up with your doctor. This can be a sign of a deficiency. Having stiff arms, hands, and legs is also abnormal. Babies are generally very flexible, so if you see that your baby is having trouble moving their limbs or bringing their hands to their mouth, this could be another sign of a deficiency.

It is unusual for any four-month-old to be silent. At this point, your baby should be babbling nonstop. If your baby has never made any noises or attempted to make any noises, this is an indication of either a speech or hearing problem. If you notice something like this, it is important to take your baby to the doctor right away.

Remember that a developmental delay, at this stage, does not necessarily indicate a permanent problem. Picking up on these signs early in your child's life will give you the chance to help them catch up. With a plan that is made by your doctor, you will be able to determine an appropriate line of action to take. Some babies develop slower than others, while some need special therapy in order to catch up. No matter what the case is, by noticing these little things, you are doing your best as a parent to give your child a wonderful life. While you don't have control over these delays, you have control over how you take action and find solutions for them.

How To Help Development

Talk to your baby all the time. This is something that has been stated from the beginning, but your baby is so close to forming words at this point. Though they might not understand everything that you are trying to express, your tone and volume will give them many context clues to pay attention to. If you do notice your baby saying something simple, such as "mama" or "dada," encourage this by repeating it. They will feel encouraged when they hear you saying the exact same thing back to them. Of course, this is a huge milestone in your baby's life, and it might even bring tears to your eyes when you hear them speak for the first time.

When a person walks in the room whom your baby is familiar with, refer to them by name. This will create even more familiarity. Now that your baby is getting so close to speaking, their ever-expanding memory will make a note of each person's name that you teach them. Pretty soon, they will be able to recognize their grandparents, siblings, and other loved ones by name. You can do the same thing with toys, objects, and food. It is never too early to teach your baby these things. When they are able to learn what everything is called, their vocabulary will be full of knowledge and information on how to ask for what they want and express how they are feeling.

Read books to your baby often! Picture books that contain bright illustrations are the best for capturing your baby's attention. Not only will this help your baby cognitively, but it will also help their physical development (by being in a seated position) and their vision. Now is the time to become a little bit more active during play sessions. Truly engage with your baby and play with toys that move or have moving parts. You will want to encourage them to explore how things work and how there are plenty of other cause and effect lessons for them to learn. Along with this, tummy time should still be a regular occurrence. You can place objects just beyond their reach to encourage crawling. You'll find that your baby will try harder to reach for the item, maybe even scooting.

Fifth Month

Milestones

Achieved Milestones:

- Sitting with slight support
- Regularly rolling over from back to tummy
- Responding to sounds
- Making a few consonant sounds
- Tongue growing more sensitive to tastes
- Showing curiosity toward stationary objects
- Communicates in response to basic expressions
- Flexes legs during tummy time
- Tests cause and effect
- Recognizes familiar faces regularly

Emerging Milestones:

- Sitting without support
- Rolling over from back to tummy and vice versa

- Responding to their name
- Making sounds with more consonants
- Learning to taste solid foods
- Tracking moving objects
- Uses sounds and expressions in conjunction
- Uses knowledge of cause and effect for more complex actions
- Tries to communicate with known people

Development

Cognitive: You will find that your baby is more captivated than ever before. By tracking objects and people, you will notice your baby observing before expressing a reaction. This is the most simple display of thinking before acting. Just as easily as your baby can become fascinated, they can also become distracted. Since their vision has improved immensely in the last few months, they are going to notice shiny, colorful, or interesting things. You might find that your baby is playing one minute and then staring at something else that has caught their eye the next. On the topic of colors, your baby should begin to start showing preferences for certain colors. This is another indication that they recognize the differences between colors. By now, your baby also has a mini vocabulary full of repetitive, mono-consonant sounds.

Physical: It is unlikely that anything will slip from your baby's hands unless they intentionally drop it. Your baby's muscles and grip should be very strong now. They will pick up objects when they want to, potentially even reaching out of their way to pick things up. Make sure that everything around your home is fully babyproofed! During tummy time, your baby will support themselves on their elbows while also lifting their chest off the ground. This is the precursor to being able to crawl. Paired with upcoming leg movements, your little one is almost mobile. Your baby is going to have a lot more say in what they want to do with their body. From sitting to rolling from their tummy to their back, they will go where they want to go.

Social/Emotional: You should clearly be able to read your baby's emotions on their face. Along with smiling, your baby should also be frowning, showing an indication of being surprised, making curious glances, and crying when they are feeling fearful or unsure. There might be some heightened anxiety when it comes to strangers, but as long as you make the introduction seem less intimidating and more joyful, your baby will start to feel more comfortable around new people. Your attitude and energy are the main things that your baby will learn from. You are setting an example for them to follow the actions that you choose. You'll learn that this is a common pattern when it comes to parenthood. You will have to utilize it often.

Is Your Baby Healthy?

Even when you are not directly addressing your baby, if you are nearby, they should turn their head to look over at you. If you notice that your baby doesn't seem to respond to the sound of your voice unless you are in front of them, this could be due to some sort of hearing impairment. You can test your baby's hearing by walking over to different parts of the room and saying their name to see what their reaction is. Also, make sure that your baby is reacting to you. Your baby should feel keen on giving you love and excitable expressions. If your baby is showing no reaction at all, this is definitely abnormal and should be brought up with your doctor.

At this age, body control is a very big milestone that should have already been accomplished. If your baby is stiff or appears very wobbly, then something is likely wrong with their muscle development. This can also be an indicator of certain autism spectrum disorders. While you cannot diagnose these things yourself, it is important that you bring them to your doctor's attention right away. The sooner the issue is addressed, the sooner you will have an answer and a solution. While it can be scary to find that your baby is behind with their development, it is much better to get a concrete answer than to worry over something that is potentially going to pass.

As stated, your baby should be a babbling machine. From cooing to expressing mono-consonant sounds, your five-month-old should be on the verge of talking any day now. This is why it is unusual if your baby is particularly quiet, and it could be the first indication of a speech impediment. It isn't realistic to expect your baby to be saying full words or sentences, but you should know that your baby is getting closer and closer to this point. While it can be unsettling to discover that your baby is extra quiet, the good news is that speech therapy can often correct these things. The earlier that you discover there is a problem, the better chance there will be for your baby to catch up on the developmental spectrum. Again, this isn't something that you can diagnose by yourself, but your doctor can provide you with more insight.

How To Help Development

Increase the amount of tummy time that you are giving your baby. A fun way to engage them is by placing all of their favorite toys around them during tummy time. You will watch as your baby giggles and rolls around, trying to get to each one of their treasured items. This is a great way to promote movement and even more muscle development. Keep speaking to your baby, as well. Even if you do not think that your baby is listening, they are. Subconsciously, your baby is receiving all of this information from you, and once they are able to process it, they are going to be talking up a storm. Explain what you are doing, as you are doing it. Point to places and things and say their names. This is going to give your baby a headstart on building up a fantastic vocabulary.

Make reading a regular occurrence, as well. Reading bedtime stories is a great way to bond with your little one. Basic stories with lots of colorful pictures will keep your baby engaged and then get them feeling sleepy enough for nighttime. Some books come with textured pages and are more interactive. These are also great to introduce to your five-month-old. The more senses you can work on, the better. Try to encourage your baby to explore each book, even if they aren't meant to be touched for textural purposes. Allow them to feel the paper and the cover of the book. If they try to put it into their mouth, gently guide them away from it and show them that it is for reading, not eating.

When you notice that your baby is putting toys in their mouth, this is likely pretty adorable and you shouldn't have a reason to stop them. However, there are potential dangers present when you allow your baby to put everything into their mouth. For example, if you are playing outside, you don't want your baby to pick up a handful of rocks and try to eat them. Teach them what is mouth-appropriate and what is off-limits. You don't have to be hard on your baby with a mean tone, and always remember to use positive reinforcement. This means that you need to focus on when they do something great and then gently guide them to a better action when they are doing something incorrectly.

Sixth Month

Milestones

Achieved Milestones:

- Can eat select fruits and vegetables
- Sits without any support
- Can use all fingers to hold objects
- Regularly practices basic cause and effect
- Makes simple vowel and consonant sounds
- Rolls in both directions
- Stretches often to reach for objects
- Sleeps for several hours through the night
- Better color, vision, and depth perception

Emerging Milestones:

- Can eat more fruits and vegetables

- Learns to get into the sitting position on their own
- Can use finger and thumb to hold items in a pincer grasp
- Can utilize cause and effect for complex actions
- Communicates through gestures and faces
- Will start to make more complex sounds
- Will roll into various positions like sitting and crawling
- Will start crawling to reach and grasp objects
- Will have even more sleep through the night with fewer feedings
- Can identify a wider range of colors and depth perception

Development

Cognitive: Your reactions will now be tested by your six-month-old in the form of cause and effect. If they throw a toy, they will be able to gauge the results by your reaction and by no longer being able to play with it. More curious than ever, your little one is starting to put these concepts together in a way that makes sense. You will notice a more vocal baby as well! Your little one should be able to make basic sounds, such as "ah" and "eh." You will also notice more imitation. This is due to the rapid rate of brain development that is happening. Even if your baby cannot speak or fully understand sentences, they should be responsive to their own name. Calling their name should cause a turn of the head.

Physical: At six months, your baby has great depth perception and color vision. They will be able to tell the difference between two different shades of the same color, and might even begin to show a preference. Their hand-eye coordination will also be improved. They will be able to hold objects, observe them, and then choose to perform an action if necessary. At six months old, your baby's back muscles are strong. They should be able to sit up without any support. You will also notice an improvement in their neck muscles. When you pick them up, their head won't fall back as easily as it used to. Another perk to these newly developed muscles is the ability to roll over in either direction, whether on the tummy or back.

Social/Emotional: A big social milestone is the ability to respond to others' emotions. If you are upset, you can expect your baby to appear concerned or upset as well. If you show them joy and elation, they will likely mirror this response. They should also be making unique vocal noises to indicate different requests. For example, a hungry noise should sound different than general fussing noise. Your baby should be inclined to play with you when you engage them. There is often nothing that an infant loves more than getting interactive with a primary caregiver. Keep playing with your baby, and encourage family group play. This will allow for even more socialization. Infants associate familiar faces with warmth, comfort, and food, so this is why your baby is so keen on you.

Is Your Baby Healthy?

If your baby tends to stay either stiff or droopy, this is abnormal for this developmental stage of life. Their muscles should be helping them greatly by now, not hindering them. If you notice this kind of abnormality in the way that their muscles are forming, this could be an early indication of some kind of physical developmental delay. Make sure that this stiffness or droopiness isn't causing them any pain if you do notice it, and tell your doctor about the issue right away.

A quiet baby can be relatively normal, depending on their personality, but a silent baby brings up a cause for concern. Differentiate if your baby is being quiet by choice or because they do not know how to begin communicating. Not responding to any sounds or noises, not even their name is another red flag. This can indicate that something isn't processing mentally, or perhaps there is a hearing impairment that is preventing them from responding.

At six months old, your baby should visually respond to you when you enter the room. By their giving you a smile or expressing a vocal sound, you should be able to tell that your baby can recognize you. It is abnormal for a baby to go without any reaction whatsoever after seeing a parent or another familiar face walk into the room. They should typically be responsive to new people walking in. A lack of reaction can indicate that they have early vision problems or perhaps some sort of cognitive delay.

Babies can be clumsy and rough when they play with their toys, but there is a difference between this and having poor motor skills. Pay attention to your baby's ability to grip objects. If your baby is given a selection of toys in front of them, they should be able to deliberately pick up the toy that they want and play with it without issues. If they cannot avoid dropping objects or just seem to be unable to reach for objects, this might be an early indication of a problem. Test your baby's motor skills by directly handing them toys and then observing what they do with them. If the object immediately falls, then you can assume something is probably wrong with their grip.

How To Help Development

Help your baby develop by including conversations into play sessions. As you are playing, explain what is happening and what each object is. Your baby will become familiar with these terms, and they will get an understanding of how everything relates. When they do begin speaking, they will already have these words in their vocabulary, which will put them ahead. Plenty of parents love to baby-talk their little ones, and it can be hard to resist, but they will not learn how to speak properly unless you speak to them first. All of the knowledge that they get at the beginning of their life is coming directly from you and the activities that you provide them.

Do some more outdoor exploration! Put your baby in the stroller and take frequent walks around your neighborhood, possibly visit some parks. This is another way to expand your baby's experiences in an educational and fun way. Point out various objects and name them so your baby understands what they are seeing. It can be a lot for a little one to process, and it might even leave them feeling worn out by the time you get back home. They will likely love this change in scenery, though. With so much to look at, your baby won't get bored.

At this point, your baby can be introduced to some solid foods. This is a huge milestone! Be careful when you introduce new foods to your baby because you aren't going to be sure about what they are allergic to if they are allergic to anything. Make sure that everything you give them is cut up into small pieces in order to avoid a choking hazard, as well. It helps to make a note each time you let your baby try something new for both the purpose of learning their preferences and also ensuring that they do not have any food allergies. You are now at a point where you can share meals with your baby, and this is a very exciting milestone for both the parent and the child. A balanced diet is still very important, so don't go crazy with junk food. Your baby might be delighted at the little taste of a cookie, but you still need to ensure that the food you are giving them is nourishing.

Chapter 6: 7th Month- 9th Month

This time period is known as the third trimester of the first year of life. Your baby has done a lot of physical and mental growth in the last few months. Compared to what they were able to do merely a few months ago, looking back on their progress should amaze you. As a parent, you have every right to feel proud of your baby and what they have learned so far. This is only the beginning because, in these next few months, the learning is only going to be expedited.

Seventh Month

Milestones

Achieved Milestones:

- Uses voice to express emotions
- Can understand the word "no"
- Can discover partially hidden objects

- Develops raking grasp
- Responds to their own name
- Can place weight on arms during tummy time
- Continues to test cause and effect
- Can identify vocal tones
- Explores objects by using hands and mouth

Emerging Milestones:

- Can make simple consonant sounds
- Understands one-word instructions
- Can completely uncover hidden objects
- Develops a pincer grasp
- Can remember the names of certain objects
- Attempts to lift the body with arms during tummy time
- Can remember the results of certain actions
- Improved ability in judging distances
- Uses hands more to manipulate objects

Development

Cognitive: If you place a favorite toy under a blanket, your baby should understand that the toy is now partially hidden. It can become a fun game of hide-and-seek as they attempt to uncover their toy. Every new object that they are given is typically going to be examined visually, as well as with their hands and mouth. Babies love to put everything in their mouths! This is a phase that you need to watch carefully, as they can often end up eating things they aren't supposed to. If you place your baby in front of a mirror, they should understand that they are seeing themselves in the mirror. This activity can provide endless hours of fun as your baby explores new facial expressions and gestures.

Physical: When you hold your baby, any weight that is placed on their legs should immediately be followed by their leg muscles kicking in as if they were about to stand on their own. This is a great sign when you notice your baby can attempt to put weight on their legs and feet. This means that walking is going to happen soon! Their raking grasp is now their preferred method of handling objects. It involves picking up items using all of their fingers, but their grip should remain solid. Since your baby has the complete ability to see all colors now, you might find them fascinated on a daily basis by the objects that they see around them. Allowing them to play with colorful toys and read colorful picture books will also enhance this curiosity.

Social/Emotional: When you tell your baby no, you should be doing this with a stern tone. You don't need to be particularly mean or authoritative, but your baby is going to acknowledge that this means they are doing something wrong. Immediately provide them with a corrected behavior that they can perform so they can understand what you want from them. This is an example of positive reinforcement, which works very well on infants. Your parenting style is up to your own preferences, but positive reinforcement tends to produce great results. At this point, building up a social circle is important. Try to get your baby involved in as many social interactions as possible. Playgroups can be a great option for you.

Is Your Baby Healthy?

The main warning sign to look for in the seventh month of your baby's life is the inability to bring their hands to their mouth. Not only is this a norm for babies of this age, but it is also an essential skill that is necessary for being able to eat. If you notice that your baby never explores this option, then you can try to show them that it is a possibility by bringing their hand up to their mouth for them. You can do this during feeding time as well as playtime. See how they react to this, and if there is still no response, you might need to discuss this with your doctor. This is an essential activity for a baby of this age to accomplish, so the sooner your baby is able to do it, the faster your baby will develop.

A lost gaze while looking around can also be concerning. Most seven-month-olds are very attentive and curious, no matter where they are or what there is to see. Staring off blankly into space can indicate some sort of a cognitive delay. Perhaps your baby just isn't processing their surroundings. You can also test this by standing beside or behind your baby and making various noises to get their attention. Call out their name, and see if you can get them to appear interested. Even the most simple gesture of returning your smile is a sign that your baby is able to process what is happening, and then react appropriately based on how they are feeling.

The same as last month, if your baby's body appears either stiff or floppy, this can mean that there is something wrong. If your baby is having tummy time, they should have the ability to roll around and move their limbs freely. The same can be said if your baby is on their back. If there isn't any movement at all or any attempt at movement, there is likely something that is preventing your baby's mobility from developing. By now, they should have plenty of muscles developed in order to assist them with this movement.

A modulation in voice is important for a seven-month-old. This is how they are able to express different emotions to you and let you know what they need. If your baby can make sounds, but they all seem monotone, this can be an issue that you should bring up to your doctor.

How To Help Development

Assist your baby in doing sit-ups. This is going to work on the development of their essential core muscles. Placing your baby into a vertical position, you can then help them up into a half-seated position. Gently placing them back down, you can do this several times to encourage them to lift their bodies up on their own. You can also encourage self-feeding. When you place your baby's food in front of them and they are hungry, they are going to make an effort to grab the food and eat it. By taking a step back and allowing them some independence, you will help them realize that they no longer need to rely on you to get fed.

At seven-months-old, you should still be providing your little one with plenty of tummy time. You can do this at least three times each day with a minimum of five minutes per session. If you notice that your baby keeps lifting their body weight onto their arms, this is a great sign! Your little one will soon be crawling all-around your home. You can place toys all-around your baby during tummy time to also encourage more reaching, a fun and interactive form of playtime.

As mentioned, social time is very important for an infant of this age. If you cannot get involved in a playgroup, try to find some friends who have children around the same age. Getting to interact with other babies will boost their social development, and it is the fastest way to get them to learn how to be social without your direct guidance.

Be selective with the toys that you get for your baby. There are certain toys that are meant to enhance comprehension skills, and these are the ones that will be best for this developmental stage. Any toys that are interactive or require a bit of a puzzle are going to be great for your little one's brain development. It will also lessen the chances of your baby getting bored or growing tired of the toys they usually play with. A challenge can be fun for a baby. You can be interactive with them at first, showing them what the objective is. They will likely catch on super quickly. Babies learn through imitation, so when they see you playing with the toy, they will want to mirror your action.

Eighth Month

Milestones

Achieved Milestones:

- Can support weight on both legs when placed upright

- Tracks moving objects
- Can manipulate objects by passing them between hands
- Can speak simple words starting with M, D, and B
- Understands basic repetitive instructions
- Develops a pincer grasp
- Displays separation anxiety
- Can easily get into a crawling position
- Understands the purpose of personal objects

Emerging Milestones:

- Can stand when holding onto support
- Tries to catch moving objects
- Develops finer control of each finger
- Improves on the range of spoken words
- Can understand a wider range of instructions
- Uses the correct noun when addressing parents ("mama" vs. "dada")
- Can use the entire hand to grasp objects
- Appears more at ease about separation

- Understands the purpose of other household objects

Development

Cognitive: Your baby might be talking now! Though the words and syllables spoken will be fairly simple, they are getting one step closer to full communication. A permanent state of curiosity is normal for an eight-month-old. They love to see how things work and like to know what you are doing. When you provide them with basic instructions, such as to put something down, they should be able to listen to you and obey. If an object is dropped in front of them, they should have no trouble keeping track of its path, and they also might reach out in an attempt to grab it. Pointing is also a new milestone that has probably been achieved. If they see something of interest, they might point to it while vocally exclaiming.

Physical: If a sound is heard from any direction, near or far, you can expect your baby to physically turn toward that sound. They should display an interest in wanting to know where it came from. Another new physical development is the mastering of the pincer grasp. This is the grasp that allows them to hold objects between their index finger and thumb. As you can imagine, this is a very useful grasp that can assist with eating and picking up smaller items. Though they might not have any teeth yet, you will notice your baby-making chewing motions with their jaw—this is a great development! Coordination is another big improvement. From passing things back and forth between hands to being able to stand with support, you will notice a lot of progress.

Social/Emotional: If your little one needs to spend time away from you, they might start to display signs of separation anxiety. This means that they might be extra fussy until they are able to see your face again. This behavior is normal at this age because you have bonded so much. Because of this, there might also be a newfound shyness when it comes to meeting strangers and accepting new people into their life. Try to encourage them as much as possible by being friendly with the individual as well. They should learn to mirror your behavior. Empathy is also something that will be learned by now. If they see or hear another infant crying, they might start crying too. This shows that your baby is developmentally on track in social situations.

Is Your Baby Healthy?

At an age where your baby should be standing with support, it is very concerning if your baby cannot sit up with or without support. When you try to prop your baby up and there is no sense of muscle control, this is an indication that they likely do not have enough muscle mass to hold themselves up. While this can be corrected, it is important to discuss it with your doctor in order to develop a plan. This will also ensure that there isn't a more serious developmental issue happening. Plenty of babies can develop neuromuscular disorders, and if they are caught early enough, there are ways that you can assist them.

Your baby should be delighted to see a familiar face, but if it appears that they cannot recognize people who should be very familiar by now, then a cognitive issue might be taking place. This is especially alarming if your baby appears to not be able to recognize your own face. Babies who do not recognize familiar faces have delays in development, and this can lead to a socially detached attitude as a result of their shortcomings. If you notice that your baby does seem drawn especially inward, this needs to be discussed with your doctor right away. There is a difference between having a shy personality and not being able to recognize faces that should definitely be familiar by now.

As time goes on, a silent baby is a big sign that something is wrong. An eight-month-old should definitely be babbling away at all times and using their vocal cords often. Even if no words are being spoken yet, attempts should be made.

If you find that your baby is just quiet, then there is likely something that is preventing them from being able to make noises. Experiment with their ability to vocalize by showing them a range of their favorite objects and foods. Your baby might appear visually excited, but if there is still no ability to make any noise, then there is likely a problem occurring internally. There are many instances when speech therapy can help your little one find their voice, so don't become overly concerned until you discuss the issue with your doctor. They will be able to come up with a proper treatment plan.

How To Help Development

Have plenty of interactive play sessions! This can be done one-on-one or in a group setting. No matter what toys you are playing with or what games you are playing, talk to your baby while this is happening. This is going to both stimulate their interest in the play session as well as encourage them to be more expressive. All around, you should notice that your baby wants to be more expressive with their body as well as the sounds that they are able to make. You might even experience some high-pitched squeals of delight as your baby experiments with their vocal range.

When you are referring to individuals and objects, refer to them by name. This is going to give your baby a better sense of what everything is and who they are interacting with. When they start talking, they will already know these words which will take out a bit of the frustration that babies can experience when they are trying to find the right words to describe things. Your baby is never too young to learn about object-noun association, so don't let their age hold you back from teaching them.

Make reading a regular activity. Whether you are reading throughout the day or before bedtime, reading to your baby is an excellent way to expand their mind. Not only do they get to see intriguing images in picture books, but they also get to listen to you reading them the story.

Having these multiple stimuli is very helpful to a developing baby, and it can make them quite happy to sit down and have these reading sessions with you.

Try to play games that encourage crawling. During tummy time, place some objects in front of your baby, just beyond their reach. This might cause some frustration, but it will also encourage them to get up and moving in order to reach their toys. Make sure that you are giving them plenty of positive praise and encouragement as they try to hold their weight up and get to these objects. The more that you do this during tummy time, the more your baby will realize that they have to take action in order to get what they want. It is a big lesson to learn in a fun way.

Ninth Month

Milestones

Achieved Milestones:

- Crawls for short distances and then sits

- Stands with support regularly
- Can say "mama" and "dada"
- Understands the word no
- Copies simple gestures
- Holds and drops objects at will
- Has favorite toys
- Moves objects from one hand to the other
- Gets nervous around new people

Emerging Milestones:

- Can crawl faster at longer distances
- Can take a step with support
- Will speak more basic syllable words
- Can interpret simple words such as "yes" and "come here"
- Will pass you an object when requested
- Will have favorite toys and people
- Can put objects into a container
- Gets nervous or shy around strangers

Development

Cognitive: Understanding the word "no" is a very big milestone. This is the beginning of your obedience training, and when your baby can correctly respond to this, you should feel very proud. Not only does this indicate that your baby trusts you and respects you, but this is also going to keep them safe. When your baby sees something interesting or unique, they will continue to use their fingers to point even more than before. They might also be pointing to indicate that they want you to bring them this object. Another way babies might use pointing is to show you that they recognize a favorite or familiar person entering the room. Pointing can lead to a very positive response from your baby, and you should encourage it.

Physical: The pincer grasp should be getting stronger, as your baby attempts to grip things strongly between these two fingers. You might even feel a cheeky pinch on your skin when your baby realizes that the grasp can be used to get your attention. An infant who is now likely crawling will also return to a sitting position on their own frequently. This position should be strong and balanced, with no wobbling. Their leg muscles are also stronger than ever, and they should be standing with assistance a lot at this age. While their upper body might be a little bit wobbly, it will soon catch up as your baby learns how to walk! This is a very exciting time in physical development for both the parents and the child.

Social/Emotional: At nine months old, it is normal for your baby to be particularly attached to you. After all, you spend the most time together. This can result in a clingy phase where your baby seems to show no interest in being held by other people or socializing with new people. This is only a temporary phase, but a lot of parents secretly enjoy it because it just shows how strong your bond is with your baby. This being said, your baby might appear more nervous around strangers than usual. As long as you keep introducing them to new people and encouraging interaction, your baby should grow out of this shyness. Be patient with your little one during this time because it is new for them as well. This behavior should never be punished or scolded because this could send a confusing message to your child.

Is Your Baby Healthy?

Nine-months-old is a very monumental age. You should have experienced many milestones by now. As a parent, trust in your ability to determine when something seems wrong with your child because you are usually correct. If your baby has not mastered sitting or crawling by now, this is definitely something that you should be concerned about. While most nine-month-olds are preparing to take their first steps, your baby is considered to be very behind developmentally if they cannot sit down or crawl without assistance. Know that this is not your fault, nor your baby's fault. Sometimes, these developmental delays just happen. There are often links to the delays in the form of disorders or defects, but with your doctor's help, you will be able to help your baby manage them.

Make sure that your baby is practicing standing up as much as possible. It is okay if they do not feel comfortable doing this on their own so much, but with your assistance, they should be okay to stand up for moderate periods of time. If this seems difficult or impossible for your baby, then there is likely something wrong. By now, your nine-month-old's leg muscles should be more than strong enough to hold up their entire body weight. If it appears that the muscles are underdeveloped, bring this up to your doctor at your next appointment.

Handgrip is a very important aspect of development. It has been discussed a lot throughout this guide, and it should be stressed that your nine-month-old should have a variety of different grips by now. From grabbing objects with their entire hand to using select fingers, there should be no issues with the strength of their grip. As they get older, the weaker their grip is, the more of a problem this presents. If your baby cannot hold onto anything, they are going to struggle as they enter the standing/walking stage and the stage where they are able to feed themselves. Keep an eye on this, and ensure that your little one has enough grip strength to perform basic necessary actions. You might need to work with your baby on certain games or activities that promote holding onto objects. Throwing a ball back and forth is one example of a game that will allow your baby to practice gripping. Feeding them finger foods often is another way to help.

How To Help Development

The best way to encourage your baby to develop is to encourage all different types of playtime. Play one-on-one with your baby, allow them to entertain themselves, find other infants for them to interact with and have regular family play sessions. Use games and toys while you play. Also try the alternative—playing with only the imagination. The more that your baby gets to experience in these final months of infanthood are going to shape them tremendously. They will turn your baby into a smart and well-rounded toddler who is ready to take on the world.

All parents want what is best for their children. While you might be feeling particularly protective over your little one, especially if they are in a clingy stage, you need to allow them to explore new places. Take them on short trips, even if only 10 minutes away from home. Show them the grocery store and the mall. These different journeys might seem very mundane to you, but to your baby, they are all going to be learning experiences. From the sights they will see to the people they might interact with, outings are a very great part of contributing to your baby's development.

Read plenty of books to your baby. You can continue to read picture books, but also try reading books that require your baby to rely solely on their imagination. You'll probably find it harder to keep them engaged with a book that doesn't have brightly colored pictures, but they will listen if you keep your tone interesting and the mood lively. Allow them to feel the textures of a book, the pages, and covers. Show them that books are special and that it is not okay to tear books. You might have to rely on your use of the word "no" here.

Continue to have conversations with your baby. You don't have to tell them your life story, but do talk about meaningful and simple things, like feelings and what is going on today. They will begin to understand more complex words and sentence structures. Pretty soon, they'll be responding to you in full sentences! This is why it is important to start early; your baby understands more than you think. You will be able to gauge their feelings by their level of vocal expression and enthusiasm when you speak to them.

Chapter 7: 10th Month-12th Month

These are the final stages of infanthood—your baby's last three months until they turn one year old. Many parents wonder where the time has gone during these last few months. While it certainly does move quickly, your baby is still going to be teaching you new things every single day, even as a toddler. This is the final transition between infant to young baby, and you will learn about all of the final milestones that will be reached during this time. As you become familiarized with what to expect, remember to also enjoy what is happening at the moment. Your baby's milestones should fill you with pride because you helped them reach every single one.

Tenth Month

Milestones

Achieved Milestones:

- Crawls and pulls to stand
- Understands some words
- Moves from tummy to sitting position
- Understands requests
- Imitates basic actions
- Searches for hidden objects
- Reacts to scary or distressing situations
- Has some teeth

Emerging Milestones:

- Walking with support (cruising)
- Understands and speaks simple words
- Can sit from standing position
- Repeats activities after observation
- Remembers the location of objects by memory
- Can have around eight teeth by their first birthday

Development

Cognitive: Object permanence is one of the biggest cognitive milestones reached by this age. This means that your baby realizes that objects continue to exist, even when hidden under blankets or other objects. When their toy disappears behind a wall in the next room, they should not throw a fit thinking that their toy is now gone forever. Because of this, your baby should feel slightly less anxious when you have to walk out of the room. They should have an understanding that you are always going to come back to them.

Another benefit of having object permanence comes with the enhanced ability to search for hidden items. Hide-and-seek games will likely become a favorite for your baby. Without upsetting them, you will now be able to hide all of their favorite toys and then watch the joyous reactions as they are all found. Your baby should now also take initiative when you hand them a picture book. While it might be hard to flip through the pages, they should be engaged as to what is going on in the book. A lot of books that are designed for babies come with hard, chew-proof pages. These are essential for your developing 10-month-old.

Physical: It is likely that you've had to barricade nearly every room in your house by now. Your baby should be crawling all over the place! Let them crawl, and let them continue to build these essential muscles in their body. Another new physical development that you might have noticed is boredom with tummy time. Instead of throwing a fit, your baby can now simply switch from being on their tummy to being in a sitting position. Of course, this puts them at an advantage to either pull up into a standing position or to begin crawling. It is a much more independent experience than it used to be.

An exciting part about your baby standing is the instances in which they feel comfortable enough to attempt to take some steps. This is one thing that you cannot rush. Your baby will feel physically ready to do this, and you need to make sure that you have your camera ready! Those first steps happen after a whole lot of exploration and a rush of bravery. They might be wobbly, but they will improve over time.

Social/Emotional: Your baby likely knows now that waving can be used as a gesture to indicate that someone is either coming or going. Waving hello and goodbye should be a regular habit by now, and it is one that forms by you waving to your baby on a regular basis. Make sure to indicate whether you are coming or going by choosing the appropriate "hello" or "bye-bye" in order for your baby to fully understand the concept. You might even find them waving at strangers during your outings, another brave step toward socialization.

Along with all of the social progress that is made this month, there comes a great deal of anxiety. Sometimes, it is normal for your baby to go through this overly-anxious phase. They might be particularly wary of strangers and unwilling for you to leave them for long periods of time. This is definitely something that they will grow out of, and you must continue working with your baby to show them that they can trust both you and the people around you. This can take a great deal of patience on your behalf.

Is Your Baby Healthy?

Your baby having some teeth is likely going to be one of the biggest changes that you will experience this month. Having some teeth assists your baby with eating, and shows that their overall development is going well. If your baby has absolutely no teeth and no indication of teeth coming in by now, then you might need to discuss this with your doctor. The average 10-month-old has at least a few teeth emerging from their gums. The potential of having a dental problem might be a setback for your baby as you try to introduce more finger foods into their diet. This problem can also eventually lead to a nourishment issue, preventing your baby from getting all of the proper vitamins and nutrients needed for a growing infant.

Dental health is very important. A lot of people underestimate this for both themselves and their children. It is best to stay on top of your baby's dental health from an early age instead of worrying about fixing it with painful and expensive surgeries later on in life. Of course, fixing dental problems as soon as you notice them also means that your baby won't have to live in pain or with uncomfortable symptoms. You will know if this is happening if your baby is reluctant to eat or refuses to allow you to open their mouth to look at their gums/teeth.

Failure to recognize people who are definitely familiar faces in your baby's life becomes even more alarming at this age. This is a clear indication that your baby either has vision problems or cognitive difficulties. For the former, this can typically be corrected fairly easily if it is a routine case of poor vision. Some babies have this gene, and they do need to wear glasses. It is not uncommon to see an infant or toddler wearing glasses, so don't feel ashamed if this is what it comes down to for your little one. Of course, the latter is a bigger problem that needs to be diagnosed by a doctor. It is impossible to tell if there are truly cognitive issues going on unless given a proper examination.

Being unable to stand, even with a lot of support, is a problem. But being unable to crawl is an even bigger issue. As you know, your baby should be well into their crawling phase by now. In fact, it is usually hard to *not* get your baby to crawl due to their constant bursts of energy and curiosity. If your baby does not show interest in crawling, you need to determine if it is physically possible to do so. When you put them into a crawling position, does it seem like they are experiencing any pain? They will likely move out of the position or move awkwardly if there is any pain being caused.

Try to assist your baby as much as you can, but know that you should not have to be assisting them very much at this age. Their independence should definitely be kicking in by now, and if it isn't, then you need to monitor them for potential delays and difficulties. No matter what, a 10-month-old should go through daily periods of being very active. If they are unusually calm or immobile, then you need to have a conversation with your doctor right away to discuss the potential problems that need to be handled.

How To Help Development

Give your baby space! Having enough space to move around is going to encourage more movement. If you can, section off certain areas of your house that allow your baby ample crawling space. Make sure they also have things to hold onto in case they want to experiment with supported standing and taking some steps. The area should be flat and level, and it should ideally be soft in case of any falls. If you have hardwood flooring, this can be slippery. You might need to put a pair of slip-free socks on your baby or place some blankets down on the floor to prevent them from getting hurt. Try not to layer too many blankets because this can also pose a potential risk of tripping your baby. One single, large blanket should do the trick. Rugs also work very well.

Get your baby at least one toy that calls for some pushing action. These toys are usually in the form of cars that have handles on the backs to give your baby a chance to stand with support. By walking forward, still utilizing this support, your baby will make the car go forward. This is an excellent way for them to develop additional muscle strength and to get them one step closer to walking on their own. Let them have regular time with this walking toy each day. The more you let them practice, the quicker they will develop the necessary skills.

At this point, you should not be baby talking to your 10-month-old. There is a difference between expressing verbal affection and baby talking. When you are affectionate, you can use your tone and attitude to show your baby your love. There is no need for any "goo-goo" or "ga ga" to do so. This will only become a setback. Use full sentences and speak properly, no matter what you are saying to your baby. Try to encourage meaningful conversations daily. Your baby is going to comprehend these things, and though the words might not be there just yet, they should respond to you in the best way that they currently know-how.

Introduce your little one to new foods. Try to offer your baby a little bit of whatever you are eating during meal times. This will expand their palette while also giving them opportunities to practice feeding themselves. You should have a set of infant utensils for them to use when the foods are not finger foods. Be aware that you should not introduce too many new foods at once for food allergy purposes. Do this with one food at a time, and if your baby has an allergic reaction, you will be able to easily narrow down which food caused the reaction.

To improve your baby's nurturing abilities, play games that encourage your baby to show their nurturing side. You can do this by playing with baby dolls and showing your baby how to take care of a younger child. Though it seems early to explore these skills, they are very important for the future. Surprisingly, a 10-month-old is very capable of having these nurturing abilities and should enjoy displaying them. You can also do things like hand your baby a comb and ask them to brush your hair. Though this is a more simple display of nurturing, it still falls into the same category. Being a great caretaker is an important skill for every individual to have.

Eleventh Month

Milestones

Achieved Milestones:

- Can stand without support

- Walks with support
- Follows basic instructions
- Manipulates objects through nimble fingers
- Knows the names of their toys
- Repeats easy and small words
- Has a wider range of foods eaten
- Can spot a familiar face in a group of strangers
- Displays frustration by babbling

Emerging Milestones:

- Will take steps without support
- Can understand complex instructions and commands
- Will develop sharp finger control with a wide range of motion
- Will remember relations to relatives
- Can remember the names of household objects
- Will repeat complex words
- Gets vocal about frustration

Development

Cognitive: Your little one should now be able to identify people by hearing the mention of their name! This means that if your baby has a grandparent who is active in their life, hearing "grandpa" will surely cause a reaction. Your baby is going to understand who this person is and what you are saying about this person. Playing with toys also changes during this month. Your little one will find new uses for toys, advancing in the way they play. They should be particularly keen on building and destroying. This shows them how things are made and what it takes to put them back together. It is a great developmental tool for them to utilize, so encourage this kind of play if you notice it. Alternatively, your baby might also be ready for precise and gentle playtime. This can include objects that are more fragile or difficult to play with, such as puzzles.

Physical: Your baby should become great at utilizing their fingers. Instead of awkwardly bending them to try and grasp their utensils, you might notice a more purposeful grip than before. The same can be seen in the way that they pick up their toys and other objects that you place in front of them. By 11-months-old. it is average for your baby to have around four teeth. This typically includes upper and lower central incisors. With these new additions, your baby is able to eat harder food items. Teething is bound to become an issue, so make sure that you have some pain-relief toys handy. A frozen teething ring feels great on your baby's sore gums. You might notice some additional fussiness due to teething, and this is normal; it will subside soon.

Social/Emotional: If your baby is around a group of strangers, they will be able to spot familiar faces in the crowd. You might even get a verbal calling out of the person's name or title as your baby realizes that they know someone. This is the month where they begin to break out of their shy phase and social anxiety. Encourage them to spend time with familiar people often. This will allow them to continue on a great path to having excellent social skills. Tantrums are another social change that you might notice, so get ready! When your baby is this smart, yet cannot express their feelings with words, they might begin to throw more tantrums. You might also notice additional babbling when they are frustrated. This is all leading up to their big milestone of turning one year old.

Is Your Baby Healthy?

A flourishing vocabulary is the sign of a healthy 11-month-old. Your baby should be on the verge of being able to tell *you* a story, so the lack of uttering even a single real word is concerning. Speech therapy might be necessary in order to get your baby caught up on the milestones that they should have reached by now. Another possibility is that there is a cognitive issue preventing them from being able to process the words that they know and turn them into vocal sounds. Consult your doctor for an opinion on the next step you should take if your baby appears to be incapable of speech.

There is a difference between having a defiant child and a child who does not understand basic instructions. An 11-month-old should be able to hand you an item at your request. If it appears that your baby does not understand your request, or ignores you, this isn't necessarily a sign that you have an unruly child. Your baby might be experiencing a cognitive delay that is preventing them from fully grasping this concept. It is another reason why you should always be conversing with your baby and explaining what things are. Talk to your doctor if you feel that your baby is developmentally behind in this area.

If your baby has poor or delayed senses, this is going to serve as a red flag to you. When you call your baby's name from behind them, this should cause an immediate reaction. Your baby's head and body will turn in unison as soon as they realize that they are being called. If you notice any type of lag between your baby hearing their name and then their reaction to being called, this could be an indication of some issues impacting their ability to fully utilize their senses. The same conclusion can be made if your baby sees an object falling and has a slight delay when trying to reach out to grab it.

With all of the encouragement that your baby has been given, standing should be mastered by now. Though they might not be able to stand on their own, a supported standing position should be regular and normal. If you notice that your baby still cannot support their own body weight, even given plenty of support, this is an indication of a physical developmental delay. Perhaps their muscles are not strong enough to make them feel secure enough to attempt a supported standing position. Discuss this with your doctor if it appears concerning.

How To Help Development

Though it seems early and it might be hard for you, encourage independence. Let your little one feed themselves and attempt to put on their own socks and shoes. This is how they are going to learn! While you will always be there to help them throughout their childhood, and even into adulthood, you need to let them learn how to do things on their own. You might notice bouts of frustration, but let your baby see if they can work through them on their own. If you notice true distress, you can insert your help and show your baby how it's done.

When you tell your baby bedtime stories, experiment with making up your own stories. Use their name, and names of familiar people, to create characters for your story. Try to keep your baby engaged by using simple situations and environments that they will understand, but tell the story directly to them as if you are a narrator. This is a different way to encourage the use of imagination, and it will help your baby explore these new elements of creativity.

Continue utilizing positive reinforcement whenever you can. If your baby does something great, let them know! A reward does not always have to be given, but praise and attention can amount to the same thing in certain cases. Your baby is never going to know right from wrong if you do not make an effort to address the differences. In positive reinforcement, punishment is not encouraged unless absolutely necessary. When possible, correct your baby instead of immediately punishing them. By showing them an alternative solution to good behavior, they will learn a lot faster with a clear mindset. If they are punished or scolded frequently, they might not realize why they are being punished in the first place.

Keep allowing your little one to socialize with other children frequently. As your baby grows older, they are going to be reaching a stage where they crave interaction with other children their own age. While interacting with you is very beneficial, there is something about interacting with other children that will teach them different social lessons. They will have to learn how to share and how to communicate with a limited vocabulary. As they play with others, you will also get to take a look at their natural temperament. Some babies are calm while others are more high-strung, and this is normal. Learn how to work with your baby's unique temperament in various social situations.

Twelfth Month

Milestones

Achieved Milestones:

- Pulling up to stand
- Taking some steps alone
- Speaking simple, single words
- Imitates actions and gestures
- Mimics sounds
- Remembers last-known location of objects
- Uses index finger to point and poke

Emerging Milestones:

- Gets into a standing position without support
- Walks for longer distances alone

- Can speak using simple phrases
- Remembers gestures and performs them on their own
- Can understand complex instructions and requests
- Remembers sounds and their sources
- Can grasp and lift objects
- Develops good hand-eye-feet coordination

Development

Cognitive: If your baby knows that their toys are normally stored in a toy box, they will automatically go to the toy box when they are ready for playtime. The associations will be made with other items around the house. For example, your baby might know that the shampoo is located in the bathroom and will be able to bring it to you upon request. They will also have a much stronger noun and object association. This means you can show your baby a bowl of fruit, and they should be able to identify which fruit you are requesting them to hand to you. These concepts should be very strong and easily understood by a 12-month-old. Imitating actions and gestures will also be very popular this month, so be careful how you present yourself! Your little one will want to be just like you.

Physical: Letting go is one of the most exciting physical developments that your 12-month-old can display. This means that they are comfortable and balanced enough to stand, unsupported, and take a few steps on their own. While they might be unsteady, these steps mark a very big milestone that officially shows you that you no longer have an infant. This is the beginning of the toddler stage, and it only continues to get faster from here. Your little one is likely going to have three pairs of teeth by now, able to eat a wide variety of foods and have a strong bite. Due to their improved vision, your 12-month-old will also have great coordination improvements. They will be able to better judge distance, as well. The index finger will be one of your baby's main tools to poke, point, and prod.

Social/Emotional: If your baby sees something that they interpret as scary, they will cry or scream. Being able to sense fear and have a personal understanding of what is scary is a huge social milestone to accomplish. This shows that your baby knows how to listen to their gut instinct. This is the age when your baby will try testing your limits. While they clearly know the difference between right and wrong, they might push your buttons to see what kind of reaction you will display. Your patience will be put to the test, but know that you are in charge! Remain firm with your positive reinforcement parenting strategy, but also know that there are certain instances when you are going to need to reprimand your little one. You will have to use your best judgment as a parent.

Is Your Baby Healthy?

There are several red flags that you can look for when determining if your 12-month-old is healthy and on the correct developmental path. One of the biggest signs to look for is their ability to sit, crawl, and stand. If they are having difficulties with any of these tasks, then they are likely developmentally behind their peers. A 12-month-old baby should have plenty of strength to get into all of these positions unsupported. If you do help them into the position, they should be able to remain in it in a sturdy fashion. While they might not be walking regularly just yet, taking a few steps is a great sign that their body is allowing for this next stage of development. A 12-month-old who is developmentally behind won't even be able to let go during a supported standing position.

The amount of talking and babbling that your child is able to do will always be a determining factor regarding their overall health. If your baby still cannot manage to form words or associate words for certain objects, then a cognitive delay is highly likely. At this age, you should be able to communicate with your baby with them having an understanding of what is being said. In turn, they should also be able to communicate back to you. Whether they use words, sounds, or expressions, communication should definitely be happening on a regular basis.

A baby who doesn't or cannot use their fingers properly would be a concern at this age. Babies at this age should be able to feed themselves if you place finger foods in front of them. With the help of infant utensils, they should also be able to have enough hand-eye coordination to use those. If your baby still doesn't seem to take any initiative when you place food in front of them, it might be due to the fact that they do not know how to eat. Some babies might display a lot of joy and excitement when given food, yet if they do not begin eating it, there might be a delay preventing them from knowing what to do next.

Overall, you need to look for any signs of independence. Your baby is one now, and this is a huge milestone! Babies at this age love to babble about things that they care about, express their feelings, try new foods, show you their favorite toys, and spend time with their loved ones. If your little one is abnormally quiet or slow, lacking enthusiasm, then you should bring this up with your doctor. There should be many ways that your baby is becoming more independent by now.

How To Help Development

Play games that encourage your baby to learn new skills! The telephone game is a favorite. Using a toy phone, pick it up and pretend that you are on a call. Your baby is likely very used to you speaking on the phone normally. They might have even tried to grab a hold of your phone before. After your conversation, pass the toy phone to your baby and tell them that someone would like to talk to them. Encourage them to speak into the receiver and have a "conversation."

Teaching your baby about sounds and where they come from is important. Allow your little one to experiment with music. Whether you get them toy instruments or simply allow them to bang on pots and pans with wooden spoons, you will likely receive a response of delight when your baby realizes that they can control what noises come from which actions.

Building with blocks is also a great mind-booster. Your baby will have to determine which pieces fit together, and through their own creativity, they will be able to build a tower of their choosing. The colors and shapes are also great for their visual and mental stimulation. Make sure that you get the blocks that are pinch-free and big enough to not become a choking hazard. Always encourage your baby when they show you their finished masterpieces.

Chapter 8: 10 Mental Leaps in Your Baby's Life

A mental leap refers to a milestone that your baby experiences mentally. Many of these mental leaps can be seen throughout the first year of life, and it becomes a joy to experience them with your baby. This chapter is going to explore the various mental leaps you can expect to see and what you can do to encourage them all. While your baby is supposed to go through these mental leaps naturally, it always helps to have a primary caregiver who is one step ahead and encouraging them. If you know that a particular leap is coming up, you can guide your baby in the right direction. As much as you would like to lead them directly into each mental leap, know that you can only do so much. Your guidance is all it takes, and then your baby will be able to figure out the rest naturally.

Mental Leap 1

This week is known as the week of changing sensations, and the name certainly suits the feelings that your one-month-old is likely having. During this first month, you have watched your baby grow faster than you could have imagined. Your baby's vision is still in soft focus right now, and you might notice a few curious gazes as they look around while trying to make sense of the world. The new sensations that your baby experiences during this first mental leap have to do with their metabolism. Since your baby relied on the umbilical cord for nutrition, they must now learn how to digest their own food. This is a very big change, so don't be surprised if your baby spits up a lot of breastmilk in the first month; it is normal.

Another way that your baby is utilizing their senses more comes from the way that they are able to remain more alert when they are awake. If they sense movement or hear noises, you might notice that they are looking around and listening to what is going on. This is a big observational phase in your baby's life, but it is a great sign that their senses are all developing as they should be. Your baby already had all of these senses present inside of the womb, but they now have a reason to use them. In the outside world, there are many more stimuli present. If your baby ever looks bewildered, it is likely that they are simply experiencing a sense from a different perspective for the first time. This is a mental leap that you might not be able to notice right away, but your baby definitely feels it.

Mental Leap 2

At around eight weeks, your baby is going to begin experiencing the world in a new way. They will begin to recognize patterns, and the things that are happening around them will start to make more sense. For example, if you put them into a feeding position, they will automatically open their mouth because they know that this means food is coming. It takes these little steps to make the bigger picture of what exactly is happening in your baby's life. At this age, your little one might make the first discovery of their hands and feet. If this happens, you can expect a lot of kicking and punching, just as they used to do in the womb.

Lights and shadows will also be of interest. Since your baby's vision is improving daily, they will better be able to see these things. You might notice your baby staring at details for longer periods of time. If you take them on an outing, they might be fascinated by the way that the grocery store is set up, with so many objects on display to observe. Your baby might start to make a few sounds at this age. You will notice some grunting and basic vowel sounds coming from your little one's mouth. When they discover their voice, they will probably experiment with it a lot. Babies this age love to see how loud they can get and what noises they can create. You might even notice some fits of giggling.

Mental Leap 3

At 12 weeks, your baby's movements should be smoother and more intentional. There will be less jerking and jumping. They are realizing exactly what they can do with their body and what it takes to move it. Though this milestone won't be reached overnight, you should notice it gradually during this mental leap. This tends to be what parents notice most at this point in their baby's development. It can be very exciting to see that your baby is experiencing more physical progress because this shows that they are discovering something new about themselves every single day.

Because of this physical leap, they will also typically experience a new cognitive leap— the ability to acknowledge exactly where sounds are coming from. Whether these noises are happening around them or nearby, your baby will be less startled by these noises and more curious. This all becomes a part of the organization that your baby is starting to develop. Events and situations will seem more purposeful and less random as they continually realize where they stem from. With this sense of a constant flow being present, your baby is beginning to mentally process where they belong in the world. Show your baby new things, slowly. Changes that are too sudden can still appear very overwhelming to an infant at this age. Introduce basic objects, perhaps some toys. New faces are also going to be interesting to your baby. The more that you can show your baby, the faster it will help them reach their next mental leap.

Mental Leap 4

Your baby now has an enhanced sense of familiar events. For example, adults know that if a ball is bounced, it is going to come back up. Babies are easily distracted and fascinated by these seemingly simple events because they have yet to fully grasp this concept. During this mental leap, your baby is going to piece some of these things together. Events become more predictable, and this is a soothing feeling to an infant who is still trying to figure out exactly how the world works. This is why a baby might cry when you leave the room; they are only beginning to find out about object permanence and concepts that are similar.

With this newfound discovery, your baby is likely feeling more confident than ever. They might begin to experiment with certain outcomes. For example, if they throw a toy down, they will wonder if it is going to come back or remain out of reach until you hand it back to them. Your baby is going to figure this concept out very quickly, and you should definitely feel very proud of your little one for making this discovery. Continue teaching them these valuable lessons, and console them when they appear to be crying in confusion. Show them that the toy will be returned to them and that you will come back into the room. While not all things are so certain, you can reinforce the concepts that are more concrete, as mentioned above.

Mental Leap 5

This mental leap marks a time of bravery! Your baby will continue to attempt to experiment with cause and effect. Watching closely, you'll notice that your baby will feel more confident with themselves and the events going on around them. Exploring their hands and feet should be a regular occurrence. They might also begin biting various objects, even if they are not edible. Babies learn best by having first-hand experiences, so allow your little one to undergo these various tasks that involve trial and error. Certain things might make them irrationally upset, but they will become less fussy the more they are able to learn.

Your baby should be around the age where they begin crawling, or at least getting into a crawling position. Mobility is a huge mental leap that happens around this time! The coordination of their arms and legs becomes very apparent, even when they are having tummy time or lying down on their back in the crib. Another significant mental leap that your baby will have is the concept of distance. This creates a radical change in perception, one that adults often take for granted. If your baby sees that a toy is out of reach, they will do what they can to indicate that they want it. They might grunt, make other noises, or attempt to reach for it. Around six months old now, your baby should be developing a unique personality that truly makes them an individual.

Mental Leap 6

At nine months old, your baby should experience yet another mental leap. This one makes your baby quite observational. When they are on the floor, they might pick up small objects and hold them tightly for examination. This tends to happen a lot when you begin feeding your baby finger foods. You might notice that a little bit of playtime happens during meals because these small pieces are going to be very intriguing to your baby. Though, they will also simultaneously understand that this is food and they can eat it. You might have to watch them closely during meals to make sure they are getting nourishment as well as entertainment. Don't be surprised if they tend to get messier; it's a fun stage!

At the same time, your baby will begin to categorize frequently. While they might be squishing their bananas and crumpling their spinach leaves, they will still realize that both of these items are food items. The same can be said for their toys, familiar people in their lives, and places that are frequented. By becoming more keen on categorization, this will help further develop all of their other senses. They will be touching more, tasting more, and hearing more. The entire world will appear even more vibrant and exuberant than it once was, and when your baby is in a good mood, you will know it. There is nothing better than the sight of a delighted nine-month-old! Get ready for even more vocal noises, too. Your baby should love attempting to put words together.

Mental Leap 7

You are now the parent of a vivacious 11-month-old, very close to the milestone of turning one! Babies are great at making messes, and they can also be great at cleaning them up if you teach them early. You might notice that mess-making is at its peak during this mental leap. Anything that you give your baby, you can expect it to be returned disassembled or changed in some way. This is how your baby is learning exactly what objects are made of and how they work. Toys that enhance these skills are essential for this mental leap. Giving your baby a productive way to make messes is going to be best for them and best for the parents who will have to do some reorganization at the end of each play session.

At this age, your baby will realize that they have to take steps in order to reach their goals. This can apply both figuratively and literally. If they want to get to a certain toy that is in the toybox, they might have to take out some of the other toys before they are able to reach the one that they desire. This is a great skill to have, and it is definitely one that is going to serve its purpose all throughout the rest of your baby's life. If your baby is hungry, they will know that in order to get fed, they will need to indicate to you that they want food. This can be done by asking for the food by name or potentially even rub their tummy.

Mental Leap 8

Your baby's first birthday is a significant leap on its own. This year signifies that babyhood is about to come to an end. Soon, you will be a parent to a walking, talking toddler. In a lot of ways, your baby is still going to be your baby. They will be reliant on you for basic care, but their independence should be on full display at all times. Children this age can be very resilient, insisting that they do things on their own (or at least, attempt to before you step in to help). Give your baby this time to discover what they are capable of. If you never take that step back, they will never know their true potential.

In this mental leap, your baby will realize that certain tasks require some level of decision-making. Though your baby is not in charge of how they are being raised and cared for, they will still exercise their decision-making rights when possible. They might make very careful selections regarding what toys they choose to play with or what books they request you to read before bedtime. You will definitely notice that your little one now has their very own set of likes and dislikes. These preferences make them individuals. Be proud of how far you have come; you've raised a well-rounded little human! Nonetheless, your baby should still be very keen on getting your opinions and knowing what you think about their actions.

Mental Leap 9

This mental leap happens when your baby is around 16 months old, and there are so many changes to look forward to. Assuming you have allowed your baby to play outside a great deal, their love and appreciation of nature should be shining through. Your child will realize that the outdoor contains so many possibilities that are not present in indoor spaces. They will likely be delighted to spend time underneath trees or on a walk in the stroller to look at flowers. Allow as much outdoor exploration as you can. Keeping your baby curious about the world will encourage them to try new things.

Their vocabulary should be quite impressive by this point. You might hear them saying words or phrases that you didn't even realize they know! Continue having meaningful and educational conversations with your baby. They might begin asking "why?" a lot, and this is a great expression of curiosity. Show them that you have the patience to answer all of their questions and explain all of their wonders. Imitation will also be a big mental leap. Be careful what you say and do because your baby is watching you closely. You are their biggest role model. Another change you might notice is your baby's ability to be dramatic, which can be quite hilarious. They might also become more demanding. Encourage these parts of their personality within reason, but also teach them about the proper way to behave.

Mental Leap 10

18 months old now, your baby will have a sense of flexibility and accountability for the way they react to certain situations. They will realize that they can be honest and kind or demanding and aggressive. These are all facets of their personality, and by having this awareness, you have the ability to shape your little one into a mindful individual. You might have to discipline your child a lot during this mental leap because

they will be so eager to show you all of these different sides of themselves. You must teach them that there is a time and a place for everything, but they also need to be observant of the rules that you have set in place from the beginning.

Your baby will now be able to handle the concept of systems. When you go to the grocery store, they should understand that there are people who work there and other people who are shopping there like you. If they attend a playgroup, they will form an association that this is a system of people who are familiar and friendly. Of course, there is also a system that is made up of family members—your baby's support system. Family and loved ones should be very trusted individuals in your little one's life. They will often prefer these people and have the most trust for them. Strong family relationships are beneficial to having a well-rounded toddler.

Conclusion

The joys of parenthood are apparent in each section of this guide. While babies can be unpredictable, there are certain milestones that you can prepare yourself for as a parent. Even if you don't know exactly what you are doing, your baby doesn't need to know that. They are going to be relying on you for guidance and support for the rest of their lives, especially as they are growing from an infant to a toddler. Try your best to have a confident approach to parenting, and you are bound to have a successful relationship with your baby.

From the moment that you find out you are expecting, you are likely going to feel elated and proud. It is during this moment when it truly sinks in that you are going to be a parent. Even if the baby is still only a few cells that are mingling together, they will be developing at a rapid rate of speed. Before you know it, you will be giving birth to your baby and learning about all of their unique habits and traits. From the way that they smile to their favorite foods, your tiny human is going to see you as their biggest role model. Because imitation is the sincerest form of flattery, be careful of what you say and do! Your baby is always going to be paying attention to you for guidance and examples.

Celebrate all of their milestones, and show them at any chance you get that you are proud of them. Babies love to be acknowledged in this way, and they require a lot of attention in order to build up their own self-confidence. A baby who is praised and raised with a positive reinforcement style of parenting is going to be a happy child. As soon as your baby is able to understand the concept, creating a reward system will help with general obedience. It will give your baby incentive to be on their best behavior in order to make you proud.

If you do happen to encounter any developmental delays or issues along the way, never panic. Your doctor is there to help you through them. They should be a professional you can trust, and they will be able to come up with a structured solution that you can follow to make sure that your baby is living their best life possible. Even if the developmental issues are permanent or uncertain, put some trust in your doctor that they are doing everything possible in order to make your baby feel better. The best thing you can do is pay close attention to each milestone and ensure that your baby is on track with their abilities and skills.

All children are different. It would be foolish to assume that your baby is going to wake up one morning with the perfect ability to communicate in full sentences, so understand that their development might be happening at a different rate for a perfectly normal reason. Again, your doctor can provide you with some clarity if you are unsure about this. You cannot compare your baby to other children their age because of this varied rate of development. As long as your baby does not appear to be in any pain or struggling, then you can keep them engaged in an effort to build their skills and abilities.

The number one thing to remember is to have fun! Your baby isn't going to stay little forever, and they won't always be so dependent on their caregivers. Enjoy this bonding time that you get to have with one another. Play with your baby frequently, talk to your baby in meaningful ways, and show your baby as many new experiences as you can. These are the true joys of parenthood. Though there can be challenging times, know that you will be able to work through them. No rough phases last forever, even the fussiest babies do calm down as they grow up. Believe that you are doing what is best for your little one, and give them all of the love that you have. When you parent them this way, they will mirror your actions and give you plenty of love in return.

References

Garoo, R. (2019a, September 10). 2-Month-Old's Developmental Milestones: A Complete Guide. Retrieved from https://www.momjunction.com/articles/babys-second-month-development-guide_00101929/

Garoo, R. (2019b, September 10). 3-Month-Old Baby Developmental Milestones - A Complete Guide. Retrieved from https://www.momjunction.com/articles/babys-third-month-a-development-guide_00102426/

Garoo, R. (2019c, September 10). 4-Month-Old Baby Developmental Milestones - A Complete Guide. Retrieved from https://www.momjunction.com/articles/babys-4th-month-a-development-guide_00104153/

Garoo, R. (2019d, September 10). 5-Month-Old Baby's Developmental Milestones - A Complete Guide. Retrieved from https://www.momjunction.com/articles/babys-5th-month-a-development-guide_00103315/

Garoo, R. (2019e, September 10). 6-Month-Old's Developmental Milestones - A Complete Guide. Retrieved from https://www.momjunction.com/articles/babys-6th-month-a-development-guide_00103340/

Garoo, R. (2019f, September 10). 7-Month-Old's Developmental Milestones: A Complete Guide. Retrieved from https://www.momjunction.com/articles/babys-7th-month-a-development-guide_00103344/

Garoo, R. (2019g, September 10). 8-Month-Old's Developmental Milestones: A Complete Guide. Retrieved from https://www.momjunction.com/articles/

babys-8th-month-a-development-guide_00102825/

Garoo, R. (2019h, September 10). 9-Month-Old's Developmental Milestones - A Complete Guide. Retrieved from https://www.momjunction.com/articles/babys-9th-month-a-development-guide_00103235/

Garoo, R. (2019i, September 10). 10-Month-Old Baby Developmental Milestones - A Complete Guide. Retrieved from https://www.momjunction.com/articles/babys-10th-month-a-development-guide_00103241/

Garoo, R. (2019j, September 10). 11-Month-Old Baby's Developmental Milestones - A Complete Guide. Retrieved from https://www.momjunction.com/articles/babys-11th-month-a-development-guide_00103429/

Garoo, R. (2019k, September 10). 12-Month-Old's Developmental Milestones: A Complete Guide. Retrieved from https://www.momjunction.com/articles/babys-12th-month-a-development-guide_00101960/

Garoo, R. (2019l, September 10). A Guide to One-Month-Old Babies' Milestones. Retrieved from https://www.momjunction.com/articles/babys-first-month-development-guide_00101911/

Higuera, V. (2014, June 12). Prenatal Development. Retrieved from https://www.healthline.com/health/prenatal-development

Mental Leap 1 - Wonder Week 5. (2019). Retrieved from https://www.thewonderweeks.com/mental-leap-1/

Mental Leap 2 - Wonder Week 8. (2019). Retrieved from https://www.thewonderweeks.com/mental-leap-2/

Mental Leap 3 - Wonder Week 12. (2019). Retrieved from https://www.thewonderweeks.com/mental-leap-3/

Mental Leap 4 - The World of Events - Wonder Week 19. (2019). Retrieved from https://www.thewonderweeks.com/mental-leap-4/

Mental Leap 5 - Wonder Week 26. (2019). Retrieved from https://www.thewonderweeks.com/mental-leap-5/

Mental Leap 6 - Wonder Week 37. (2019). Retrieved from https://www.thewonderweeks.com/mental-leap-6/

Mental Leap 7 - Wonder Week 46. (2019). Retrieved from https://www.thewonderweeks.com/mental-leap-7/

Mental Leap 8 - Wonder Week 55. (2019). Retrieved from https://www.thewonderweeks.com/mental-leap-8/

Mental Leap 9 - Wonder Week 64. (2019). Retrieved from https://www.thewonderweeks.com/mental-leap-9/

Mental Leap 10 - Wonder Week 75. (2019). Retrieved from https://www.thewonderweeks.com/mental-leap-10/

The Bump. (2017, June 19). 1 Month Old Baby. Retrieved from https://www.thebump.com/baby-month-by-month/1-month-old-baby

WhattoExpect. (2019b, October 8). 4 Weeks Pregnant Symptoms - Week 4 Pregnancy Signs, Cramping, Baby Development, and More. Retrieved from https://www.whattoexpect.com/pregnancy/week-by-week/week-4.aspx

www.ingramcontent.com/pod-product-compliance
Lightning Source LLC
Chambersburg PA
CBHW071910110526
44591CB00011B/1623